BIRD WATCHER'S DIGEST

Midwestern Birds

BACKYARD GUIDE

BILL THOMPSON III

COOL
SPRINGS
PRESS

Brimming with creative inspiration, how-to projects, and useful
information to enrich your everyday life, Quarto Knows is a favorite
destination for those pursuing their interests and passions. Visit our
site and dig deeper with our books into your area of interest:
Quarto Creates, Quarto Cooks, Quarto Homes, Quarto Lives,
Quarto Drives, Quarto Explores, Quarto Gifts, or Quarto Kids.

Inspiring | Educating | Creating | Entertaining

First published in 2013 by Cool Sprints Press an imprint of The Quarto Group,
100 Cummings Center, Suite 265D, Beverly, MA 01915 USA.
T (978) 282-9590 F (978) 283-2742 QuartoKnows.com

Cool Sprints Press titles are also available at discount for retail, wholesale, promotional,
and bulk purchase. For details, contact the Special Sales Manager by email at specialsales@
quarto.com or by mail at The Quarto Group, Attn: Special Sales Manager, 100
Cummings Center, Suite 265D, Beverly, MA 01915 USA.

ISBN: 978-1-59186-559-9

Acquisitions Editor: Billie Brownell
Design Manager: Brad Springer
Cover Design: Michelle Thompson
Interior Design: Mary Rohl
Layout: Danielle Smith

Photo Credits
Cover image: Brian Lasenby/Shutterstock.com
George Armistead: pp. 52
Jim Burns: pp. 46, 90
Kyle Carlsen: pp. 12, 13, 20 (both), 23, 112
Robert McCaw: pp. 40, 118, 128
Brian Small: pp. 6, 14, 42, 48, 50, 54, 58, 60, 62, 64, 66, 68, 70, 74, 78,80, 82, 84, 86,
    88, 92, 94, 96, 98, 100, 102, 104, 106, 108, 110, 114, 116, 120, 122, 126, 132, 136,
    138, 140, 142, 144, 146, 148
Bill Thompson III: pp. 8, 9, 11, 15, 18, 21 (both), 24, 25, 26, 27, 28 (both), 29, 30
    (both), 31, 33, 38, 44, 56, 76, 124, 130
Michael Williams: pp. 134
Julie Zickefoose: pp. 72

Dedication & Acknowledgments

DEDICATION

To my parents Bill & Elsa Thompson, for having the foresight to start *Bird Watcher's Digest* long before bird watching was a socially acceptable activity. And to all the many subscribers, writers, and other contributors to *BWD* over the years, thanks to you, every day I learn something new and wonderful about birds. And to the birds . . . where would we be without the beauty and wonder of birds?

ACKNOWLEDGMENTS

If you think that creating a book like this is difficult, let me tell you that you're 100 percent correct in that assumption. However, I am fortunate in having so many talented people around me, which makes the book-making process a whole lot easier.

My team at *Bird Watcher's Digest* is without peer in their ability to bring our collective ideas (or my crazy ones) to fruition, whether in print, digital, video, or any other form. Like any major-league team, our roster changes a bit from time to time, but these are the all-stars that I get to write into each day's line-up: Elsa Thompson, Andy Thompson, Ann Kerenyi, Laura Fulton, Katherine Koch, Claire Mullen, Jim Cirigliano, Michelle Barber, Kyle Carlsen, and Wendy Clark. All of these folks helped a great deal in creating this book and I thank them from the bottom of my birdy heart.

Special mention goes to Kyle Carlsen. Kyle is the assistant editor of *Bird Watcher's Digest* and a freelance writer. He received his first pair of binoculars as a gift on his seventh birthday and has been watching birds ever since. He also is the founder of Back Road Birding Tours in southeastern Ohio. Kyle was basically a co-author for this book, writing a large number of species profiles and all the material on the regional birding hotspots. There's no way I would have gotten all of this done without Kyle's help.

Finally, thank you for reading this book (or at least reading *this far* in this book). Authors cannot be authors without people to read what they've written. I hope you find the content we've created to be both useful and interesting. And more than that I hope it helps you to enjoy your backyard birds a lot more in the seasons to come. Happy backyard birding!

Bill Thompson III
Marietta, Ohio   April 2013

CONTENTS

Welcome to Bird Watching in the Midwest

Watching birds, bird watching, or birding—whatever you call it—is one of America's fastest-growing and most popular hobbies. According to a recent survey by the U.S. Fish & Wildlife Service, there are as many as *46 million* bird watchers in the United States. Back in 1978, when my family began publishing *Bird Watcher's Digest* in our living room, bird watching was still considered a bit odd. The image many people associated with bird watching was the character of Miss Jane Hathaway of the television show *The Beverly Hillbillies*. Fortunately, that stereotype is long gone now, and our culture has come to embrace bird watching as an enriching, exciting pursuit—one that can be done with little expense and enjoyed almost anywhere at any time.

WHAT *IS* BIRD WATCHING?

The dictionary defines bird watching as "the identification and observation of wild birds in their natural habitat as a recreation." But as any bird enthusiast can testify, bird watching is a lot more than mere identification and observation. It's about discovery and adventure. It's about attracting and pursuing. It's about connecting with the natural world. And it can be done right in your own backyard.

Sometimes it's hard to know who's doing the watching!

WHY DO WE WANT TO WATCH BIRDS?

Birds have inspired humans for thousands of years. Birds can fly—something we humans have mastered only in the past 100 years. Birds have brilliant plumage, and some even change their colors seasonally. Birds are master musicians, singing beautiful and complex songs. They possess impressive physical abilities—hovering, flying at high speeds, and withstanding extreme weather conditions as well as the rigors of long migration flights. Birds also have behaviors to which we can relate, such as intense courtship displays, devotion to their mates, and the enormous investment of effort spent in raising their young. Sound familiar? In short, birds are a vivid expression of life, and we admire them because they inspire us. This makes us want to know them better and to bring them closer to us. We accomplish this by attracting them to our backyards and gardens, and by using binoculars and other optics to see them more clearly in an "up-close and personal" way.

A male northern cardinal adds color to a snowy landscape.

A BRIEF HISTORY OF BIRD WATCHING

Before the arrival of modern optics that help us view birds more closely, humans used a shotgun approach to bird watching. Literally. Famed ornithologist and bird artist John James Audubon was the first European to document many of the North American bird species in the early 1800s. He did so by shooting every unfamiliar bird he encountered. Having a bird in the hand allowed him to study it closely, and to draw it accurately. This was an excellent method of learning a lot about birds quickly, but it was rather hard on the birds. This method of bird study continued largely unchecked until the early 1900s, when the effects of market hunting on birds became unhappily apparent. In 1934, a young bird enthusiast and artist named Roger Tory Peterson published *A Field Guide to the Birds*, with a system of arrows showing key field marks on the plumage of each species. This enabled a person to identify a bird from a distance, with or without the aid of magnifying optics. Modern bird watching was born, and it was no longer necessary to shoot birds in order to positively identify them. The era of shotgun ornithology was over.

BIRD WATCHING TODAY

Bird watching today is about seeing or hearing birds, attracting them when possible, and then using certain clues to positively identify them. To reach this identification, we use two important tools of the bird-watching trade: binoculars and an identification book. The binoculars (or perhaps a spotting scope, which is a telescope specially designed for nature watching) help you to get a closer, clearer look at the bird. The field guide or other identification book helps you interpret what you see so that you can identify the bird species.

We live in the golden era of bird watching. When I started birding more than 40 years ago, feeders, seed, birdhouses, and other supplies were hard to come by—we had to make our own. Now they are available in almost any store. We can buy a field guide or a book like the one you're holding in any bookstore. We can try out optics at camera stores, outdoor suppliers, bird supply stores, and even at birding festivals (for those who really get into bird watching). We can learn about birds in special bird courses, on the Internet, in magazines, or from DVDs and videos. We can join a local or state bird club and meet new bird-watching friends. We can even take birding tours to far-off places. There's never been a better time to become a bird watcher. So let's get started!

HOW TO GET STARTED:
BASIC GEAR, EQUIPMENT, AND TECHNIQUES

If you're just starting out watching birds, you may need to acquire two basic tools—binoculars and an identification guide—and you've got the second one already!

Binoculars and Other Optics

You may be able to borrow optics from a friend or family member, but as your interest takes off, you'll certainly want to have your own binoculars to use anytime you wish. Fortunately, a decent pair of binoculars can be purchased for less than $100, and some really nice binoculars can be found used on the Internet or through a local bird club for just a bit more. Check out the tip at right for magnification requirements.

Try to find binoculars that are easy and comfortable to use. Make sure they focus easily, giving you a clear image, and that they are comfortable to hold (not too large or heavy) and fit your eye spacing. Every set of eyes is different, so don't settle for binoculars that just don't feel right. The perfect pair of binoculars for you should feel like a natural extension of your hands and eyes. Over time you will become adept at using your optics and, with a little practice, you'll be operating them like a pro.

> **SEEING CLEARLY**
>
> Magnification powers commonly used for bird watching are 7x, 8x, and 10x. This is always the first number listed in the binoculars' description, as in 8 x 40. The second number refers to the size of the objective lens (the big end) of the binocular. The bigger the second number, the brighter the view presented to your eye. In general, for bird-watching binoculars the first number should be between 7x and 10x, and the second number should be between 30 and 45.

Select binoculars that feel good in your hands and are easy to use.

A field guide is one of birding's most essential tools.

Identification Guides

When choosing a field or identification guide, you'll need to decide what type of birding you'll be doing and where you plan to do it. If nearly all of your bird watching will be done at home, then this book is a great introduction! Or, you might want to get a more advanced field guide to the backyard birds of your region, or at least a field guide that limits its scope to your half of the continent. Many field guides are offered in eastern (east of the Rocky Mountains) and western (from the Rockies west) versions. This book, of course, is just for the your part of the country and is naturally more specific to your region. But geographically limited formats include only those birds that are commonly found in that part of the continent, rather than continent-wide guides that include more than 800 North American bird species. If you decide to get a field guide too, choose one that is appropriate for you, and you'll save a lot of searching time—time that can be better spent looking at birds!

Getting to Know the Birds in Your Backyard

Most people who watch birds start out at home, and this usually means getting to know the birds in your backyard. A great way to enhance the diversity of birds in your yard is to set up a simple feeding station. Even a single feeder with the proper food can bring half a dozen or more unfamiliar bird species into your yard. And it's these encounters with new and interesting birds that make watching birds so enjoyable.

Start your feeding station with a feeder geared to the birds that are already in your backyard or garden. For most of us this will mean a tube or hopper feeder filled with sunflower seeds. Place the feeder in a location that offers you a clear view of bird activity, but also offers the birds some nearby cover in the form of a hedge, shrubs, or brush pile into which the birds can fly when a predator approaches. I always set our feeding stations up opposite our kitchen or living room windows because these are the rooms in which we spend most of our daylight hours, and because these rooms have the best windows for bird watching. We'll discuss bird feeding and attracting in greater detail in the next section.

Once you've got a basic feeder set up outside, you'll need to get yourself set up inside your house. You've probably already selected the best location for viewing your feeder. Next you should select a safe place to store your binoculars and field guide—somewhere that is easily accessible to you when you suddenly spot a new bird in your backyard. At our house we keep binoculars hanging on pegs right next to our kitchen windows. This keeps them handy for use in checking the feeders or for heading out for a walk around our farm.

Hanging a suet feeder is a good way to attract woodpeckers.

BEYOND THE BACKYARD

Sooner or later you may want to expand your bird-watching horizons beyond your backyard bird feeders and bird houses. Birding afield—away from your own home—can be a wonderfully exhilarating experience. Many beginning bird watchers are shy about venturing forth, afraid that their inexperience will prove embarrassing, but there's really no reason to feel this way. The best way to begin birding away from the backyard is to connect with other local bird watchers via your local bird club. Most parts of North America have local or regional bird clubs, and most of these clubs offer regular field trips. Bird watchers are among the friendliest people on the planet, and every bird club is happy to welcome new prospective members. If you don't know how to find a local bird club, ask your friends and neighbors if they know any bird watchers, check the telephone directory, search the Internet, or ask at your area parks, nature centers, and wild bird stores.

Getting out in the field with more experienced bird watchers is the fastest way to improve your skills. Don't be afraid to ask questions ("How did you know that was an indigo bunting?"). Don't worry if you begin to feel overwhelmed by the volume of new information—all new bird watchers experience this. When it happens, relax and take some time to simply watch. In time you'll be identifying birds and looking forward to new challenges and new birds.

Away from feeders, mockingbirds eat a variety of berries, insects, or spiders.

A daily bird notes diary.

KEEPING A LIST

Many people who become more interested in bird watching enjoy keeping a list of their sightings. This can take the form of a simple written list, notations inside your field guide next to each species' description, or notes in a special journal meant just for such a purpose. There are even software programs available to help you keep your list on your computer. In birding, the most common list is the *life list*. A life list is a list of all the birds you've seen at least once in your life. Let's say you noticed a bright black-and-orange bird in your backyard willow tree one morning, then keyed it out in your field guide to be a male Baltimore oriole. This is a species you'd never seen before, and now you can put it on your life list. List-keeping can be done at any level of involvement, so keep the list or lists that you enjoy. I like to keep a property list of all the species we've seen at least once on our 80-acre farm. Currently, that list is at 186 species, but I'm always watching for something new to show up. I also update my North American life list a couple of times a year, after I've seen a new bird species.

TEN TIPS FOR BEGINNING BIRD WATCHERS

1. Get a decent pair of binoculars, ones that are easy for you to use and hold steady.

2. Find a more advanced field guide to the birds of your region (many guides are divided into eastern and western editions). Guides that cover all the birds of North America contain many birds species uncommon to or entirely absent from your area. You can always upgrade to a continent-wide guide later.

3. Set up a basic feeding station in your yard or garden.

4. Start with your backyard birds. They are the easiest to see, and you can become familiar with them fairly quickly.

5. Practice your identification skills. Starting with a common bird species, note the most obvious visual features of the bird (color, size, shape, and patterns in the plumage). These features are known as field marks and will be helpful clues to the bird's identity.

6. Notice the bird's behavior. Many birds can be identified by their behavior—woodpeckers peck on wood, kingfishers dive for small fish, and swallows are known for their graceful flight.

7. Listen to the bird's sounds. Bird song is a vital component of birding. Learning bird songs and sounds takes a bit of practice, but many birds make it pretty easy for us. For example, chickadees and whip-poor-wills (among others) call out their names. The Resources section of this book contains a listing of tools to help you to learn bird songs.

8. Look at the bird, not at the book. When you see an unfamiliar bird, avoid the temptation to put down your binoculars and begin searching for the bird in your field guide. Instead, watch the bird carefully for as long as it is present—or until you feel certain that you have noted its most important field marks. Then look at your field guide. Birds have wings, and they tend to use them. Your field guide will still be with you long after the bird has gone, so take advantage of every moment to watch an unfamiliar bird while it is present.

9. Take notes. No one can be expected to remember every field mark and description of a bird. But you can help your memory and accelerate your learning by taking notes on the birds you see. These notes can be written in a small pocket notebook, in the margins of your field guide, or even in the back of this book.

10. Venture beyond the backyard and find other bird watchers in your area. The bird watching you'll experience beyond your backyard will be enriching, especially if it leads not only to new birds, but also to new birding friends. Ask a local nature center or wildlife refuge about bird clubs in your region. Your state ornithological organization or natural resources division may also be helpful. Bird watching with other birders can be the most enjoyable of all.

A QUICK GUIDE TO GETTING STARTED

Welcome to the wonderful world of bird watching! To get you started, let me explain how to use this book. The featured birds are in order *taxonomically*—that is, how you'd find them in a bird identification book. That's so we can group birds that are in the same family together—the robin and wood thrush, for example. It will help your identification process to have similar birds closer together so you can flip from one page to another to double-check the photograph.

Each featured bird includes a large photograph, usually a male in breeding plumage, as its identification shot. Bear in mind that female birds and juveniles often have drabber coloring. I've described those in each profile. The topics that most bird watchers want to know are covered:

- **How do I identify it?** This is a physical description of each bird and ways to distinguish it from other similar-looking birds.

- **Where do I find it?** This section describes the bird's preferred habitat, where you are most likely to spot it.

- **What can I feed or do to attract it?** We all want to attract birds to our backyard (well, most birds). This paragraph explains how to create the environment that the bird loves! It includes information on feeders and bird food, as well as creating a habitat with water and plants.

- **Nesting** explains where and how the featured bird builds its nest, including whether it will nest in a birdhouse.

The "At A Glance" chart quickly identifies attributes of the featured bird that will either help you identify it or attract it. An "✔" in the column indicates that the feature applies to the bird in question.

Now—let's get going!
Bill Thompson III

AT A GLANCE

🏠	✔	Uses a birdhouse
⛲	✔	Visits bird baths
🪣	✔	Attracted by feeders
🌹	✔	Attracted by specific plants
♪	✔	Has a unique call or song
🐦	✔	The female's plumage is different

Creating a Habitat
Attracting Birds to Your Backyard with Food, Water, Shelter, and Plants

Birds need four basic things to live: food, water for drinking and bathing, a safe place to roost, and a safe place to nest. Believe it or not, these four elements are actually quite easy for you to offer to birds, even if your backyard is small. A bird-friendly backyard has a good feeding station with several feeders and food types; a shallow birdbath with moving water; a variety of shrubs, trees, and other plants for adequate cover and natural nesting opportunities; and a birdhouse or two for cavity-nesting birds, such as chickadees and bluebirds. This chapter will provide you with the tools you need to transform your backyard—no matter the size—into an inviting place for birds throughout the year.

FEEDING BIRDS

Bird feeding is a good place to start your bird-attracting efforts. It's wise to begin with a single feeder, such as a hopper or tube feeder filled with black-oil sunflower seeds. The black-oil sunflower seed is the most common type of sunflower seed available because it's the seed type that most of our feeder birds can readily eat. Think of it as the hamburger of the bird world! The black-oil sunflower seed has a thin shell (easy for seed-eating birds to crack) and a large, meaty seed kernel inside. As you can see from the seed preference chart on page 22, many backyard birds eat sunflower seeds.

A single feeder with the proper food can bring half a dozen bird species to your yard.

Other excellent foods for birds include mixed seed (a blend that normally includes millet, milo, cracked corn, and other seeds), sunflower bits (shells removed), peanuts (best offered unsalted and without the shell), suet or suet cakes, cracked corn, thistle seed (also known as niger or nyjer seed), safflower seed, nectar (for hummingbirds), mealworms, fruits, and berries. Bird feeding varies from region to region—don't be afraid to experiment with new feeders or food. Birds will vote with their bills and stomachs and will let you know their preferences.

Eating the food at feeders is not the only way birds find sustenance. A backyard or garden that includes natural food sources for birds—such as seed-producing flowering plants and fruit-bearing trees and shrubs—will further enhance its attractiveness to birds. In fact, it's often the natural features of a backyard habitat that attract the birds' attention rather than the bird feeders.

Pictured from the top down: Black-oil sunflower seed, peanuts, mixed seed, and safflower seed.

A mourning dove at a platform feeder.

FEEDER TYPES

It's important to match the foods and feeders to each other as well as to the birds you wish to attract. Sunflower seed works in a wide variety of feeders, including tube, hopper, platform, and satellite or excluder feeders (which permit small birds to feed, but exclude larger birds), as well as for ground feeding. Mixed seed does not work as well in tube or hopper feeders for a couple of reasons. First of all, the birds that prefer mixed seed tend to be ground feeders, so it's less natural for them to go to an elevated feeder for food. Secondly, elevated feeder designs (such as tubes or hoppers) are built to dole out seed as it is eaten and the smaller size of most mixed seed kernels causes excess spillage. Mixed seed works best when offered on a platform feeder or when scattered on the ground.

A white-breasted nuthatch at a peanut feeder.

When purchasing your feeders and foods, make sure they will work effectively with one another. Specialty foods such as suet, peanuts, thistle (niger or nyjer), mealworms, fruit, and nectar require specific feeders for the best results for you and the birds. The Food and Feeder Chart on the next page is a great place to start.

FOOD AND FEEDER CHART

SPECIES	FOOD
Quail, Pheasants	Cracked corn, millet, wheat, milo
Pigeons, Doves	Millet, cracked corn, wheat, milo, niger (thistle seed), buckwheat, sunflower, baked goods
Hummingbirds	Plant nectar, small insects, sugar solution
Woodpeckers	Suet, meat scraps, sunflower hearts and seed, cracked corn, peanuts, fruits, sugar solution, mealworms
Jays	Peanuts, sunflower, suet, meat scraps, cracked corn, baked goods
Crows	Meat scraps, suet, cracked corn, peanuts, baked goods, leftovers, dog food
Titmice, Chickadees	Peanut kernels, sunflower, suet, peanut butter, mealworms
Nuthatches	Suet, suet mixes, sunflower hearts and seed, peanut kernels, peanut butter, mealworms
Wrens, Creepers	Suet, suet mixes, peanut butter, peanut kernels, bread, fruit, millet (wrens), mealworms
Mockingbirds, Thrashers, Catbirds	Halved apples, chopped fruit, mealworms, suet nutmeats, millet (thrashers), soaked raisins, currants, sunflower hearts
Robins, Bluebirds, Other Thrushes	Suet, suet mixes, mealworms, berries, baked goods, chopped fruit, soaked raisins, currants, nutmeats, sunflower hearts
Kinglets	Suet, suet mixes, baked goods, mealworms
Waxwings	Berries, chopped fruit, canned peas, currants, dry raisins
Warblers	Suet, suet mixes, fruit, baked goods, sugar solution, chopped nutmeats
Tanagers	Suet, fruit, sugar solution, mealworms, baked goods
Cardinals, Grosbeaks	Sunflower, safflower, cracked corn, millet, fruit
Towhees, Juncos	Millet, sunflower, cracked corn, peanuts, baked goods, nutmeats, mealworms
Sparrows, Buntings	Millet, sunflower hearts, black-oil sunflower, cracked corn, baked goods
Blackbirds, Starlings	Cracked corn, milo, wheat, table scraps, baked goods, suet
Orioles	Halved oranges, apples, berries, sugar solution, grape jelly, suet mixes, soaked raisins, dry mealworms, currants
Finches, Siskins	Thistle (niger), sunflower hearts, black-oil sunflower seed, millet, canary seed, fruit, peanut kernels, suet mixes

SETTING UP A FEEDING STATION

Place your feeding station in a spot that is useful and attractive to you and the birds. When we moved into our farmhouse, we looked out all the windows before choosing a spot for our feeding station. You may want to do the same thing. After all, the whole point of bird feeding is to be able to see and enjoy the birds. From the birds' perspective, your feeders should be placed adjacent to cover—a place they can leave from and retreat to safely and quickly if a predator appears. This cover can be a woodland edge, brushy area or brush pile, hedges or shrubs, or even a weedy fencerow. If your yard is mostly lawn, consider creating a small island of cover near your feeding station. This will greatly enhance the feeders' appeal to birds.

Be patient. You've spent the money and effort to put up feeders, but don't expect immediate dividends. Birds are creatures of habit, and it may take a few days or even a few weeks before they recognize your offering as a source of food. Sooner or later, a curious chickadee, finch, or sparrow will key into the food source, and the word will spread along the local bird "grapevine."

A tube feeder filled with black-oil sunflower seed is a great way to start your feeding station.

BIRDHOUSES

Almost every bird species builds or uses some type of nest to produce and rear its young. However, only a small fraction of our backyard birds use nest boxes provided by humans. Birds that use nest boxes or birdhouses are called "cavity nesters" because they prefer to nest inside an enclosed space, such as hole excavated in a tree, as many woodpeckers do. Nest boxes simulate a natural cavity, but they have the added advantage (for humans) of our being able to place them in a convenient spot. To the birds' advantage, we can protect the nest box from predators, bad weather, and other problems.

Birds are also attracted to nesting materials. This tufted titmouse is gathering alpaca fiber for its nest.

Being a landlord to the birds is a thrilling experience. You are treated to an intimate peek inside the lives of your "tenants" and rewarded with the presence of their offspring, if nesting is successful. To help ensure the nesting success of your birds you need to provide the proper housing in an appropriate setting, and you should monitor the housing during the nesting season.

The Right Housing

Two factors are key to providing the right nest box for your birds: the size of the housing and the size of the entry hole. Not all cavity nesters are picky about the interior dimensions of the cavity, except when it is excessively big or small. But the size of the entry hole is important because it can effectively limit the entrance of large, aggressive nest competitors, predators, and inclement weather. For example, an entry hole with a diameter of 1½ inches on a bluebird nest box will permit entry by bluebirds and many smaller birds, including chickadees, titmice, nuthatches, wrens, and tree swallows. But this same size keeps European starlings out and prevents them from usurping the box.

An Appropriate Setting

Place your nest boxes where they will be most likely to be found and used by birds. Bluebirds and swallows prefer nest sites in the middle of large, open, grassy areas. Wrens, chickadees, nuthatches, flycatchers, woodpeckers, and other woodland birds prefer sites that are in or adjacent to woodlands. Robins, phoebes, Carolina wrens, barn swallows, and purple martins prefer to nest near human dwellings, perhaps for the protection from predators that we provide.

Monitoring Your Nest Boxes

By taking a weekly peek inside your nest boxes, you will stay abreast of your tenants' activities, and you'll be able to help them raise their families successfully. During most of the year, your birdhouses will appear to be empty. This does not mean that the boxes are going unused. In fact, many birds use nest boxes during the winter months as nighttime roosts. A loose feather, insect parts, berry seeds, or a few droppings are classic evidence of roosting activity.

Eastern bluebird eggs.

During breeding season, your regular visits will help you know when nest building begins and when eggs are laid, and will give you an idea about how soon the eggs will hatch and the babies leave the nest. Bird nests are vulnerable to a variety of dangers, including harsh weather and predators such as cats, raccoons, snakes, and even other birds, as well as nest-site competitors. These dangers are greatly reduced when nest boxes are monitored because the birds' landlord (you) can take steps to protect the nest.

On my trips to check each of our ten nest boxes, I keep a small notebook with me to record my observations. Each nest box has its own name and number in my notebook, along with the date of each visit and a note about what I've found.

Carolina chickadee nestlings.

When nesting starts in a box I note the date, what materials are used to construct the nest, and the date that the first egg was laid. Once the clutch is complete and the female begins incubating the eggs, I can estimate the hatching date. This usually takes about 14 days. Another 14 to 21 days later, I know the young birds will be ready to leave the nest.

Peeking Inside

When checking a nest box, approach quietly. During the breeding season, you may scare the female off the nest temporarily when you open the box. Don't worry. If you keep your visit brief, she'll be back to the nest soon. I visit nest boxes in the late morning on sunny days, when the adult birds are likely to be away finding food. I open the box, quickly count the eggs or young, close the box and move away before pausing to record my notes. It's a myth that opening a nest box or checking the young will cause the adults to abandon the nest. In fact, over time many cavity-nesting birds that use nest boxes grow quite accustomed to regular visits.

One final note on nest monitoring. As fledging time approaches for the young birds—normally about two weeks after the eggs hatch—you should curtail your box visits to avoid causing a premature nest departure.

When Things Go Wrong

You open your nest box, and you find broken or missing eggs and the nest in disarray. What happened? The bad news is: a predator has raided your nest, and, in the natural order of things, the eggs or nestlings have been eaten. The good news is: there are steps that you can take to avoid such an event in the future.

It's important to protect your nest boxes so predators cannot easily access them. For many homeowners, the best option is to mount the housing on galvanized metal poles with pole-mounted predator baffles installed beneath the boxes. An added advantage to pole-mounting (as opposed to mounting on a fencepost or tree) is that the housing can be moved to a new location fairly easily.

You may wish to consult one of the publications listed in the Resources section for specific strategies for dealing with nest box predators and pests.

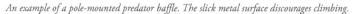

An example of a pole-mounted predator baffle. The slick metal surface discourages climbing.

CREATING A BACKYARD BIRD HABITAT

To make your backyard or garden a haven for birds, all you need to do is think like a bird. Look around your yard. Where is the food, the water? Where are the places to hide from predators or to shelter in bad weather? Is nesting habitat available?

An ideal bird habitat can be created in a tiny urban garden just as it can be created in a large rural setting. Birds

Black-eyed Susans provide food for birds.

love varied habitats, so when you are planning your yard, landscape, or gardens, resist the urge to plant matching plants in straight lines. Instead, let your imagination go wild—literally. Give the edges of beds or gardens natural curves. Scatter trees, shrubs, and vines in clumps or islands around the area you are designing. On the edges of your property, try to create natural transitions from the grass of your yard to the tops of your trees with short and medium-height plants that provide food and shelter for birds.

Edible Habitat

Birds have evolved over millions of years right alongside the native plants with which they share the planet. These same native plants can work for you in your bird-friendly habitat plan. Your local nursery, nature center, or native plant

Black raspberry plants provide a natural food source for backyard birds.

society should be able to recommend plant species that are native to your region. Native plants not only provide food in the form of fruits and nuts, but birds may also eat the plants' buds, leaves, nectar, and sap, as well as the insects that live on the plants. When choosing your native plants, select a wide variety of species, sizes, shapes, and seasonality. Planting only one or two plant species will minimize the number of birds your habitat will attract.

Water

Birds need water all year long for drinking and bathing. The best way to offer water to birds is in a shallow birdbath with about 2 inches of water in it. I've always had good luck attracting birds to water in my yard when the bath was on or near the ground and when the water had some motion to it.

The sight and sound of moving water are highly attractive to birds. You can add motion to any birdbath or water feature with a mister, dripper, or a recirculating pump. Misters and drippers attach to your garden hose and release a small amount of water that disturbs the surface of the bath; these ripples are eye-catchingly attractive to birds. Recirculating pumps, which require electricity, recycle the water from the main bath through a pump and filter and then back to the bath. If you live in an area where water freezes in winter, add a small electric birdbath heater to keep the water open and available to birds.

If you already have a water garden or water feature, consider making part of it accessible to birds. This can be accomplished by placing a flat rock shelf on or near the water's surface, or by allowing recirculating water to trickle over an exposed flat rock. Our backyard water garden is ringed with goldfinches almost every day all year round. They use a large, flat piece of slate that gets splashed by our small waterfall as a place to grab a quick drink.

Water is a universal attractant for birds—species that might otherwise never visit your yard, feeders, or birdhouses will visit a clean and alluring birdbath or water feature.

Moving water is irresistible to birds.

A male house finch rests in a raspberry tangle.

Shelter

When they need to rest, hide from danger, or get out of the weather, birds seek deep cover in the form of thick vegetation, vine tangles, dense evergreens, or brushy areas. These bits of habitat may not be first on a landscaper's list of backyard beautifying accents, but to a bird they are vital havens. Even a brush pile in a corner of your property can offer enough shelter during a storm to help sparrows, cardinals, and other backyard birds survive.

Look at your bird habitat, and observe where the birds go just before a storm or at dusk. These are the places in which they shelter themselves. Consider adding more habitat, and your yard will be even more attractive to birds.

A variety of plant types helps attract more backyard birds.

The more your backyard looks like nature, the more attractive it will be for birds.

Places to Nest

The majority of North American birds do not use nest boxes. Most build their nests in places that are hidden from view—in trees, bushes, or secluded spots on or near the ground. Some birds—such as phoebes, barn swallows, and Carolina wrens—are bold enough to build nests on porch ledges, in garages, and in barns. House finches and mourning doves are known for building their nests in hanging flower baskets, but these sites won't satisfy most of our birds.

The places where birds choose to nest are similar to the places they choose to roost and shelter—in thick vegetation and deep cover out of view of passing predators. In providing a nesting habitat for birds, the key is diversity. As you read through the species profiles in this book, notice the habitat features that each species prefers. Then factor this information into your habitat plans.

Helping Other Nesting Birds

There are many things you can do to help non–cavity nesters—all those birds that build open-cup nests and will never use one of our nest boxes. The most important thing is to offer variety in your landscaping or backyard habitat. A backyard that is mostly lawn with a tree or two staked out in the middle will not be nearly as appealing as a yard featuring a variety of plant types, including grasses, perennial plants, shrubs, bushes, trees, and other natural elements. The more your landscape looks like nature, the more attractive it will be for birds.

BIRD-FRIENDLY LANDSCAPING TIPS
FOR MIDWEST GARDENS

The Midwest region enjoys the best of all four seasons and a wide range of habitat types from the western edge of the Appalachian Mountains to the eastern edge of the Great Plains. It is bookended by the two great migratory flyways of the eastern half of the continent, the Atlantic Flyway and the Central Flyway. Here are some tips and plant suggestions for making your Midwest backyard as bird-friendly as possible:

- Plan your bird-friendly landscape for four seasons. Plant blooming plants in spring and summer, plus sheltering habitat like vine tangles, shrubs, evergreens, thickets, and hedgerows for nesting and roosting birds. Plant seed-producing flowers that bloom in late summer and provide seeds throughout the fall and winter, such as coneflowers, sunflowers, zinnias, and asters.

- Offer a source of water for bathing and drinking and a source of dry, bare or sandy earth for dust-bathing species like grouse, quail, wild turkeys, thrashers, and others.

- *Don't* rake up all the leaves in autumn. Leaf litter creates habitat for many of the terrestrial creatures that are bird food items, such as slugs, grubs, snails, spiders, and earthworms.

- If you can avoid it, don't treat your lawn with chemicals. The Midwest is the epicenter of distribution for a variety of birds that feed on open grassy areas, including American robins, eastern bluebirds, and killdeer. Chemical treatment may make your lawn more lush-looking, but they are not at all healthy for birds.

- Create shelterbelts of habitat with hedgerows, vine-covered fencerows, and weedy tangles for birds to use during harsh winter weather.

- Add these flowering plants, grasses, and vines for birds: bittersweet, purple coneflower, little bluestem, greenbrier, coral honeysuckle, trumpet creeper, Virginia creeper, poison ivy, and wild grape.

- Berry-producing plants for birds include hollies, dogwoods, eastern red cedar, junipers, wild cherry, redbud, and red mulberry.

- Some great shrubs for birds are beautyberry, devil's walking stick, elderberry, red osier dogwood, inkberry, common juniper, spicebush, and sumacs.

An example of a bird-friendly backyard: weedy edges, a nice variety of trees, flowering plants for hummingbirds, shaded areas, and well-situated viewing spots for year-round enjoyment.

- These trees are fabulous for attracing birds: American beech, northern red oak, white oak, black willow, hackberry, serviceberry, red osier dogwood, tulip poplar, pawpaw, black willow, river birch, sycamore, and red mulberry.

PLACES FOR YOU

As you plan for your bird-friendly habitat, you'll also want to incorporate elements that you can use and enjoy, such as bird-attracting plants, a water garden, benches, shady relaxation spots, and perhaps a location for your feeding station. Remember, the whole point of attracting birds to your property is so that you can enjoy them while they enjoy your offerings. Plan with your favorite viewing spots in mind, and you'll be rewarded with year-round free (and natural) entertainment.

BIRD-FRIENDLY PLANTS FOR YOUR BACKYARD

TREES		
Common Name	*Latin Name*	*Good For/Other Notes*
Apple	*Malus* spp.	Fruit, insects, nesting cavities
Ash	*Fraxinus* spp.	Seeds, insects, cover
Aspen	*Populus* spp.	Seeds, insects, cover, nesting cavities
Birch	*Betula* spp.	Seeds, insects, cover
Cedar	*Juniperus* spp.	Fruit, year-round cover
Cherry	*Prunus* spp.	Fruit
Chokecherry, Common	*Prunus virginiana*	Fruit
Cottonwood	*Populus* spp.	Nesting cavities, shelter
Crabapple	*Malus* spp.	Fruit, insects
Dogwood	*Cornus* spp.	Fruit
Fir	*Abies* spp.	Year-round cover
Hackberry	*Celtis* spp.	Fruit, cover
Hawthorn	*Crataegus* spp.	Fruit, cover, nesting
Hemlock	*Tsuga* spp.	Seeds, insects, shelter
Holly	*Ilex* spp.	Fruit, year-round cover
Juniper	*Juniperus* spp.	Year-round cover
Larch	*Larix* spp.	Seeds
Madrone	*Arbutus* spp.	Fruit
Maple	*Acer* spp.	Seeds, cover
Mesquite	*Prosopsis* spp.	Shelter
Mountain Ash	*Sorbus* spp.	Fruit
Mulberry, Red	*Morus rubra*	Fruit
Oak	*Quercus* spp.	Acorns, cover, insects
Pine	*Pinus* spp.	Year-round cover, insects
Poplar	*Populus* spp.	Nesting cavities, shelter
Sassafras	*Sassafras albidum*	Fruit, cover, nesting cavities
Shadbush (Serviceberry)	*Amelanchier laevis*	Fruit, flowers
Spruce	*Picea* spp.	Year-round cover
Sycamore	*Platanus* spp.	Nesting cavities, shelter, insects
Willow	*Salix* spp.	Nesting cavities, shelter, insects

SHRUBS		
Common Name	*Latin Name*	*Good For/Other Notes*
Arrowwood Viburnum	*Viburnum dentatum*	Fall fruit; tolerates shade
Bayberry, Northern	*Myrica pensylvanica*	Fruit; male & female plants needed for fruit
Blackberry, American	*Rubus allegheniensis*	Fruit; dense cover; nesting
Blueberry, Highbush	*Vaccinium corymbosum*	Fruit, flowers, cover; needs acid soil
Chokeberry, Red	*Aronia arbutifolia*	Fruit; moist soil preferred
Cranberry, Highbush	*Viburnum trilobum*	Fruit; shade tolerant
Dogwood	*Cornus* spp.	Fall fruit; dense cover
Elderberry, American	*Sambucus canadensis*	Fruit; dense cover
Hercules' Club	*Aralia spinosa*	Fruit
Hobblebush	*Viburnum alnifolium*	Fruit; shade tolerant
Holly, Deciduous	*Ilex decidua, Ilex* spp.	Winter fruit; male & female plants needed for fruit
Huckleberry, Black	*Gaylussacia baccata*	Fruit; sandy soil preferred
Inkberry	*Ilex glabra*	Fruit; thicket-forming; needs acid soil
Mahonia	*Mahonia aquifolium*	Fruit; year-round cover
Manzanita	*Arctostaphylos* spp.	Early fruit; thick cover
Nannyberry	*Viburnum lentago*	Fruit; shade-tolerant
Pokeweed	*Phytolacca americana*	Fall fruit
Rose	*Rosa* spp.	Winter fruit; summer flowers
Shadbush	*Amelanchier* spp.	Early fruit
Spicebush	*Lindera benzoin*	Fruit; needs moist soil
Sumac	*Rhus* spp.	Fruit available all winter
Viburnum	*Viburnum* spp.	Fall fruit; tolerates shade
Winterberry, Common	*Ilex verticillata*	Fruit; male & female plants needed for fruit
Yew	*Taxus* spp.	Year-round cover; some fruit

(CONTINUED FROM PREVIOUS PAGE)

VINES

Common Name	Latin Name	Good For/Other Notes
Ampelopsis, Heartleaf	Ampelopsis cordata	Fruit; resembles a grape vine
Bittersweet, American	Celastrus scandens	Fruit; avoid Asian species
Grapes, Wild	Vitis spp.	Fruit; cover; attracts 100 species
Greenbriars	Smilax spp.	Fruit; thick cover
Trumpet Honeysuckle	Lonicera sempervirens	Nectar; fruit; cover; avoid Asian species
Trumpet Vine	Campsis radicans	Nectar; summer cover
Virginia Creeper	Parthenocissus quinquefolia	Fruit; attracts 40 species

FLOWERS

Common Name	Latin Name	Good For/Other Notes
Aster	Aster spp.	Flowers; seeds; attracts butterflies
Bachelor's Button	Centaurea cyanus	Seeds
Black-Eyed Susan	Rudbeckia serotina	Seeds
Blazing Star	Liatris spp.	Seeds; flowers attract butterflies
California Poppy	Eschscholzia californica	Seeds
Coneflower, Purple	Echinacea purpurea	Seeds; flowers attract butterflies
Coreopsis	Coreopsis spp.	Seeds; flowers attract butterflies
Cornflower	Centaurea cyanus	Seeds
Cosmos	Cosmos spp.	Seeds
Daisy, Gloriosa	Rudbeckia cv.	Seeds
Goldenrod	Solidago spp.	Flowers for butterflies; winter cover
Joe-Pye Weed	Eupaorium spp.	Flowers for butterflies; winter cover
Marigold	Tagetes spp.	Seeds
Penstemon	Penstemon spp.	Nectar; seeds
Poppy	Papaver spp.	Seeds; flowers attract butterflies

FLOWERS		
Common Name	Latin Name	Good For/Other Notes
Primrose	Oenothera spp.	Seeds
Sedum	Sedum spp.	Seeds; flowers attract butterflies
Sunflower	Helianthus spp.	Seeds
Thistle, Globe	Echinops spp.	Flowers; seeds; nesting material
Zinnia	Zinnnia elegans	Seeds; flowers attract butterflies

INTERESTING BIRD FACTS

- A house wren can feed 500 spiders and caterpillars to its nestlings during a single summer afternoon.

- A chimney swift can devour 1,000 flying insects in a single day.

- A barn owl can swallow a large rat whole. After digesting its meal, the owl coughs up a pellet containing the rat's bones and fur.

- A Baltimore oriole can eat as many as 17 hairy caterpillars in a minute.

- Quail, sparrows, and other seed-eating birds sometimes swallow fine gravel, which they store in a special part of their digestive system. This gravel, known as grit, helps to break up hard seeds to make them easier to digest.

- More than 70 different bird species have been observed drinking nectar from hummingbird feeders.

- Starlings love to adorn their nest cavities with shiny or colorful things such as coins, bits of plastic, and other birds' feathers.

- A tundra swan's plumage contains more than 25,000 feathers.

- Herons and egrets were once shot by the thousands so that their ornate feathers could be used to decorate women's hats. The shooting of most migratory birds is now illegal.

- Peregrine falcons may reach speeds of 200 miles per hour when diving for prey. They use their balled-up talons to knock out their prey, then catch the hapless, falling bird before it hits the ground or water.

Profiles of Backyard Birds of the Midwest

In the following pages we've created a handy guide to fifty-five of the most common backyard birds of the Midwest. These include common feeder visitors, year-round resident species, birds that are present during the nesting seasons, and a few others that you're sure to encounter at some point in your yard or nearby. During the course of your bird watching, you'll probably see other birds passing through your yard that are not included here—after all there are *hundreds* of bird species that may be seen in the Midwest each year. At the back of this book there are some pages where you can record your backyard bird sightings and observations. I hope you'll enjoy these species profiles, and have some fun along the way. Happy backyard bird watching!

Sharp-shinned Hawk

If the birds at your feeder seem skittish, they have a good reason—a sharp-shinned hawk could appear at any moment. Its primary prey, after all, is small songbirds. This songbird specialist is actually doing nature a favor by weeding out the slowest, weakest, or oldest birds, helping to keep bird populations healthy. Once thought to be an evil killer of innocent birds, thousands of sharpies and other hawks used to be shot, a practice that has since been outlawed. Your first reaction to a sharp-shinned hawk in your backyard might be horror, but you have to respect the bird's ability as a predator. Watch the

hawk's intense focus when it's perched, and listen for how the songbirds warn each other about the hawk. It's like a television nature show, live from your living room window!

HOW DO I IDENTIFY IT? Sharp-shinned hawks are built for speed and maneuverability with short rounded wings, a slender body, and long narrow tail. They fly like a jet fighter as they chase fleeing songbirds into and through thick cover. Adult sharpies have reddish breasts and a dark gray head and back. Young birds have brown backs and white breasts coarsely streaked with brown. Sharpies appear small-headed and smaller-bodied when compared to the similar, but larger, Cooper's hawk. Flying sharpies almost always follow this rhythm: flap, flap, flap, glide.

WHERE DO I FIND IT? Forest habitats of almost any type are home to sharp-shinned hawks, but they are most likely to be found where songbird populations are thriving. Sharpies have a vast breeding range, but they prefer large tracts of woodland for nest sites, so they are rarely observed on the nest. In fall most migrate southward, their movement triggered by passing cold fronts. Some migrate as far as Central America, but many spend the winter in the continental United States.

WHAT CAN I FEED OR DO TO ATTRACT IT? While many people may not wish to attract a sharp-shinned hawk to their property, if you have small birds at your feeders or in your gardens, sooner or later they will attract the attention of a passing hawk. Hunting sharp-shinned hawks use surprise and speed—emerging suddenly from behind a line of trees or bursting forth from a quiet, concealed perch. As surprised birds scatter, the sharpie pursues one and grabs it with its long, taloned toes. If undisturbed, the hawk may finish its meal on the ground, or it may carry it away to a safer location. Sharpies will take prey as large as ruffed grouse and as small as hummingbirds.

NESTING The nest of the sharp-shinned hawk is usually well hidden. In fact, you are more likely to hear the adults calling to one another as they share the nesting and feeding duties than actually see them. The nest is made of sticks and is built by the female high in a tree. She lays four to five eggs and incubates them for about a month. After hatching, the female broods the young birds for about 20 days, all the while being fed by her mate. A month after hatching, young hawks are ready to leave the nest, though they spend several more weeks being fed by the parents.

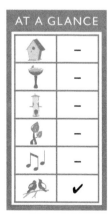

AT A GLANCE	
🏠	–
🍶	–
🗼	–
🌱	–
♫	–
🐦	✔

Cooper's Hawk

Cooper's hawks often perch in inconspicuous places, shooting through the branches or dropping from trees to nab unsuspecting prey. A flurry of fearful birds and a gray flash may mark the arrival of a Cooper's hawk to your back-yard. Cooper's hawks are medium-sized hawks and formidable hunters that are usually seen singly except during migration.

Cooper's hawks are attracted to what bird feeders attract—birds!—helping to maintain the natural balance between predator and prey, even in the suburbs. When successful, Cooper's hawks usually weed out the birds that are sick, old, or otherwise less than perfectly healthy. They will not scare birds from your feeders for very long. Soon after the hawk departs, the activity at your feeder will return to normal.

HOW DO I IDENTIFY IT? It can be a little confusing to see the difference between the Cooper's hawk and the similar sharp-shinned hawk. Adults of both species have similar markings, as do their brown-backed immatures (birds that are less than a year old). Size is often not a trustworthy identification tool in the field—proportions and tail edges are more telling. Compared with the sharp-shinned hawk, the Cooper's has a proportionately larger head and neck and a rounded (not notched) or square-tipped tail (as does the sharp-shinned). Perched, adult Cooper's hawks often show a color contrast between a dark crown and gray back. In flight, a Cooper's hawk's head sticks out well past the front edge of the wings, and the end of its tail usually looks rounded. Sharp-shinned hawks look like a capital "T" in flight, their shorter heads almost even with the front edge of their wings.

WHERE DO I FIND IT? In many areas, Cooper's hawks are uncommon nesters. Far-northern birds generally winter to the south. You can look for Cooper's hawks in any type of forest, along forest edges, and in woods near watercourses. But don't be surprised if you find one elsewhere, particularly in winter and fall. They seem to be adapting to suburban life, nesting near backyards or in city parks. During spring and fall, migrating Cooper's hawks gravitate toward ridges and coasts.

WHAT CAN I FEED OR DO TO ATTRACT IT? These hawks are not attracted to seed at feeders—they are attracted to the *birds* at your feeders. Cooper's hawks generally feed on midsized birds, including robins, flickers, doves, and pigeons, but they also eat small mammals, including chipmunks and squirrels. Insects and reptiles are sometimes featured on the menu. If you have a backyard with a bit of woodland and some active feeders, a Cooper's hawk is a likely visitor.

NESTING Cooper's hawks place their bulky stick nests high on horizontal branches in large trees, sometimes building them atop another large bird or squirrel nest. The female lays three to five eggs and incubates them for about five weeks. The male brings food, but the female feeds it to the young, which usually take flight about four or five weeks after hatching. Both adults and young birds can be quite vocal around the nest. The typical call is a loud *kik-kik-kik-kik* that sounds like an angry woodpecker.

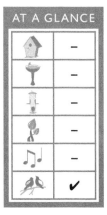

AT A GLANCE

🏠	–
🛁	–
🌿	–
🌱	–
♪	–
🐦	✔

Rock Pigeon

Originating in northern Europe, Africa, and India, rock pigeons—largely gone from their former wild haunts—have spread to cities and towns worldwide thanks to their domestication 5,000 years ago. Evidence of domestication lies in their highly variable coloration; a flock may contain birds in every color, from pure white to reddish to solid black. Rock pigeons are nonmigratory, though pigeon racing clubs worldwide exploit their celebrated homing skills. Older field guides and bird books may refer to this species as rock dove and feral pigeon. Some backyard bird watchers also refer to these birds as sky rats or feeder pigs. Why? Because they can clear out a feeder faster than a vacuum cleaner.

Thanks to pigeons' flocking habit, most homeowners are less than delighted when they visit. The most effective deterrents seem to be sturdy feeders enclosed by wire caging that excludes the larger-bodied pigeons while admitting smaller birds. Some people spread food for rock pigeons far away from the main feeding stations to keep the pigeons from overwhelming seed feeders.

HOW DO I IDENTIFY IT?   A chunky-bodied bird with a small head, deep chest, powerful wings, and a square tail, the rock pigeon is built for flight. Wild-type birds are slate blue with a white rump, black terminal tail band, and two black bars on the inside back edges of the gray wings. In bright sunlight you may see the pinkish green iridescence on the neck. Pigeons have short, reddish legs and a short, straight bill. Their song is a series of soft, resonant coos—*ooh-ga-rooogh*—and a harsh *woogh!* serves as an alarm call. Pigeons are almost always found in flocks except when tending young.

WHERE DO I FIND IT?   It is rare to find rock pigeons in natural habitats, though there are still some cliff-nesting populations in North America along rivers and rocky ocean coasts. Most rock pigeons prefer tall buildings, with their many ledges, to be ideal nesting sites. These same pigeons are happy to take food, such as bread and popcorn, from city sidewalks. In suburban areas they can be found nesting under bridges, and in rural areas, in old barns.

WHAT CAN I FEED OR DO TO ATTRACT IT?   Walking and pecking with rapidly bobbing heads, pigeons find their preferred food—grains, seeds, and some fruits—on the ground. Pigeons will eat anything that might be offered, but millet and cracked corn are special favorites. If you really wish to attract rock pigeons, toss mixed seed on the ground beneath your feeders. Urban birds have highly developed scavenging skills, raiding trashcans and fast food litter for tasty morsels of food.

NESTING   The male's spinning, bowing, and cooing is a common sight on city sidewalks. Pigeons mate for life, with the males guarding females zealously. They may lay eggs and raise young anytime. Building ledges, highway overpasses, barns, bridges, and other structures may be selected as the site on which to build a stick-and-grass nest and lay two eggs. Both males and females incubate for about 18 days. The rubbery, black-skinned squabs stay in the nest 25 to 45 days. Because they are common and accustomed to human activity, the rock pigeon is a very easy bird to see and watch. Many urban schools study rock pigeons as a part of their science classes.

Eurasian Collared-Dove

Some North American bird species are native and are beloved backyard friends. Others are like obnoxious relatives who come from far away and over-stay their welcome. The Eurasian collared-dove is one of these. A medium-sized dove that is native to Asia, the Eurasian collared-dove has spread across much of the globe, usually preferring to live in close proximity to humans. If it weren't for a messy burglary of a pet shop in the Bahamas in the 1970s, we might not have the Eurasian collared-dove as a common (and spreading) nesting bird in the New World. After its release, it began colonizing Florida in the 1980s. Today this bird is found all across the western two-thirds of North America, as far north as Alaska. In some areas its numbers have grown so significantly that it is considered a pest. Look for these doves perched on utility poles, wires, and rooftops, where its chunky, square-tailed shape is easily recognized.

HOW DO I IDENTIFY IT? The Eurasian collared-dove is larger and chunkier-looking than the familiar mourning dove and about the same size as a rock pigeon. It shares the mourning dove's pale tannish gray coloration, but where a mourning dove's tail is long and tapered, the collared-dove's is squared off at the end. Adults have a uniform black half-collar on the nape of the neck, which gives this species its name. The Eurasian collared-dove is a powerful, direct flyer and, when in flight, it shows obvious white patches in the tail. The bill is black and the legs are reddish. The call is a repetitive (and somewhat owl-like) *who-HOO-huh, who-HOO-huh.*

WHERE DO I FIND IT? The short answer is: almost everywhere. This dove is a resident throughout its range, meaning that it does not migrate seasonally as do many of our songbirds. It thrives in human-altered habitats. They are at home and equally successful in urban, suburban, and rural settings as long as there is a reliable food source available, such as a bird feeder, croplands, a grain elevator, or a farm feedlot. For most of us, we'll hear this bird before we see it, since it calls regularly all day long, especially during the breeding season. Having said that, the Eurasian collared-dove perches in obvious places, so it's not that hard to see.

WHAT CAN I FEED OR DO TO ATTRACT IT? Eurasian collared-doves are ground-feeders that eat seeds and grain for much of their diet. Their rapid spread across North America has been abetted by backyard bird feeders, and by spilled grain at silos and in animal feedlots. They need open, grassy spaces for foraging and areas of thick vegetation (medium-sized trees and vine tangles) for nesting. They will also forage in areas where weed seeds are left over after the growing season. Thanks to their adaptive nature, the Eurasian collared-dove takes advantage of almost any bird-friendly habitat you provide. This species will regularly visit a backyard water feature or birdbath.

NESTING The male calls to the female from various possible nesting sites on buildings and in trees. After she selects one, he brings her nesting materials (grass, twigs, feathers, rootlets) as she builds it. Two white eggs are laid and incubated for slightly more than two weeks. Young doves fledge about 17 days later and shortly thereafter the parents may begin another nesting cycle.

Mourning Dove

Whether you regard them as songbirds or gamebirds, if you feed birds, you probably have mourning doves as constant companions. These tapered, graceful brown and pinkish birds wholeheartedly embrace human alterations of the natural landscape. In fact, mourning doves are most common in agricultural and suburban areas. Doves love water, but may foul birdbaths by sitting around the rim, tails in, letting their droppings fall into the water. Streamlined, fast, and powerful flyers, mourning doves travel in flocks, descending to feed on a great variety of grains and weed seeds that they peck from the ground.

HOW DO I IDENTIFY IT?   The mourning dove is a slender, long-tailed bird compared to the equally common rock pigeon. They are tannish gray overall with a pointed tail that shows obvious white spots along its tapered edges. The mournful *oooahh, oooh, ooh, ooh* song of the mourning dove is a very familiar backyard sound, echoing from power lines and treetops in early spring. When startled into sudden flight, their wings make a whistling sound.

WHERE DO I FIND IT?   Like the Eurasian collard-dove, the mourning dove is found almost everywhere. The only habitat shunned by mourning doves is deep, contiguous forest. They are most common in agricultural areas with hedgerows and shelterbelts. They are often seen in ranks on power lines over farm fields. They are also abundant in suburban areas, where visits to feeding stations are an integral part of their daily routines. Mourning doves migrate, especially far northern populations, but some individuals are resident year-round.

WHAT CAN I FEED OR DO TO ATTRACT IT?   Mourning doves take any seeds that might be offered at feeders, preferring sunflower seeds, cracked corn, millet, milo, and other grains found in seed mixes. They are experts at emptying feeders and can consumer large amounts in a single visit. Afterwards it is common to see a small flock of mourning doves settle in on a nearby perch to relax while they digest their large meal. Open, grassy or weedy areas are attractive to mourning doves, which prefer to feed on the ground. They prefer to roost in dense cover, such as evergreen trees, and may also use these same trees for nesting.

NESTING   Mourning doves may mate and nest in any month of the year, but males begin to tune up their songs in late winter. They have a production-line breeding mode, following one brood with another as often as six times in a season. The twig nest platform—placed in a wide variety of tree species, but frequently in a pine—is often so flimsy that eggs show through from beneath. Two eggs are incubated by both members of the pair, and they hatch in 14 days. Young doves are fed first on crop milk, a secretion unique to the pigeon family, and later on regurgitated seeds. Young remain in the nest for another 15 days but may fledge much earlier. The male feeds them until about day 30, while the female re-nests. Immature birds are visibly smaller and have fine, buff feather edges overall. Mourning doves travel in flocks for much of the year, breaking away only to find a mate, nest, and raise young. Males defend their mates as a kind of mobile territory, defending her and the immediate nest site—but not much else—from other birds.

AT A GLANCE	
	–
	✔
	✔
	–
	✔
	–

Eastern Screech-Owl

Eastern screech-owls are very acclimated to humans, but their nocturnal habits and natural camouflage keep us from seeing them regularly. Even when perched in full view in daylight, screech-owls have a remarkable ability to conceal themselves. They are common in cities and towns, but the screech-owl's success is due not only to its secretive nature, but also to its ability to catch and eat a wide variety of small prey. This bird's name is misleading; a screech is rarely voiced. The call most bird watchers hear is a series of descending, whinnying whistles and tremolos on a single note.

HOW DO I IDENTIFY IT?   A small bird (8½ inches long), the eastern screech-owl occurs in two color variations: reddish and gray, with gray being more common. The screech-owl's mottled plumage appears very barklike. When open, the owl's eyes are large and yellow, with big black pupils. Its "ears" are really just feather tufts (the owl's actual ears are built into its skull). These can be raised or lowered depending on the bird's mood and they serve to enhance the owl's natural camouflage. When a "screech" sits with its body elongated, eyes closed, and ear tufts extended, it looks like a broken branch stub.

WHERE DO I FIND IT?   A resident bird (one that does not migrate) throughout the eastern half of the United States, the screech-owl is found wherever woodlands are mature enough to have cavities. Unlike many other owl species, the screech-owl is commonly found in urban parks and suburban backyards. You probably already have eastern screech-owls in or near your backyard. Spend some time outside at night—especially when the moon is full—listening for the screech-owl's wavering calls. Check natural tree cavities during the day for roosting or nesting owls—they may be peering out of the hole, particularly on sunny winter days.

WHAT CAN I FEED OR DO TO ATTRACT IT?   Eastern screech-owls will eat almost anything—from mice and voles to moths, earthworms, crawfish, frogs, and fish. In spring and summer, they prey upon small and medium-sized songbirds, but during winter small mammals are more common prey. Screech-owls perch in a tree, waiting and watching for potential prey, most of which is captured with the owl's feet in flight or by pouncing on the ground. You can attract screech-owls with an owl nest box. Boxes should be about 12 to 14 inches deep with an internal floor size of 7 × 7 inches and a 2¾-inch-diameter entry. Place the box more than 10 feet high in a shady spot on a tree trunk that is wider than the box's width.

Some backyard bird watchers have also reported seeing screech-owls using their birdbaths at night for bathing and drinking.

NESTING   Screech-owls nest in natural cavities and will readily use nest boxes (see above). They begin nesting early, from mid-December in the South and late March in the North. Two to six eggs are laid and a month-long incubation period ensues. The female incubates the eggs and broods the young owlets, while the male delivers all the food. Owlets remain in the nest for a month before venturing into nearby trees. They remain dependent on their parents for two months.

AT A GLANCE	
🏠	✔
🛁	✔
⚱	–
🌻	–
🎵	✔
🦋	–

Chimney Swift

Known by bird watchers as "the flying cigar," the chimney swift is a familiar sight in the sky over cities and towns during the spring, summer, and fall. Its nickname aptly describes the swift's elongated shape in flight. The twittering, chattering calls of chimney swifts are one of the most common bird sounds of summer. It is named for its preferred nesting and roosting site—the inside of chimneys. This species spends much of its life on the wing, stopping only to sleep and nest.

Allowing chimney swifts to nest in your older, unused chimney is really easy—just let the swifts find it. They pose no danger and, if not for the sounds of hungry nestlings during a two-week period, you might not know they are there. If hosting swifts is not your cup of tea, check around your town or region for chimneys being used by swifts. Watch for them entering or leaving the large brick chimneys on schools and old factories. Modern chimneys with metal caps and flues are impossible for swifts to use.

HOW DO I IDENTIFY IT? Chimney swifts are a dark charcoal-gray overall with a small black bill, black eyes, and tiny feet. Indeed, their feet are almost useless for walking but are perfect for clinging to the inside surface of a brick or stone chimney. The chimney swift is nearly all wing, with a 5-inch-long body and a 14-inch wingspan. Four hundred years ago, all chimney swifts nested in hollow trees and caves, but the arrival of European settlers and their stone chimneys soon provided abundant nesting sites. Today most chimney swifts nest in chimneys and other human structures, such as unused smokestacks and abandoned buildings.

WHERE DO I FIND IT? Widespread and common across the eastern half of the United States and southern Canada, the chimney swift is found wherever there are suitable nest sites. Fall migratory flocks of swifts are a magnificent spectacle as they form a swirling, chattering cloud descending to roost in a large chimney at dusk. In winter, this tiny bird migrates to South America, returning again in March to the southern United States.

WHAT CAN I FEED OR DO TO ATTRACT IT? An all-insect diet is captured and consumed on the wing. Swifts often are seen flying high in the sky when foraging. Reducing your use of lawn and garden chemicals will increase your chances of having the types of flying insects that chimney swifts eat. If you do not have a swift-friendly chimney, but still wish to attract these birds, consider building a swift nesting tower. Plans for such structures are available on the Internet. When built and placed in a proper habitat these towers have a very high rate of use by nesting pairs of chimney swifts.

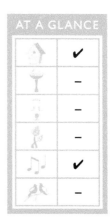

AT A GLANCE

NESTING A pair of swifts chooses a nest site—usually a chimney. The nest is a half-saucer shape made of sticks held together and made to stick to the wall of cavity by the birds' saliva. Swifts break small twigs off trees, grabbing them with their feet as they fly past a tree. Two to five eggs are laid, and both parents share incubation (15 days) and brooding duties until the young swifts fledge at about 19 days after hatching.

Ruby-throated Hummingbird

The only breeding hummingbird east of the Great Plains, the ruby-throated hummingbird enlivens many gardens with its presence. Males are fiercely combative and will defend a single nectar source against all comers. Spectacular pendulum flights, constant chittering, the low hum of beating wings, and the occasional smack of tiny bodies colliding are familiar to anyone lucky enough to have rubythroats in their gardens or at their nectar feeders.

HOW DO I IDENTIFY IT?   Seen in direct sunlight, the male's ruby throat patch—called a gorget—dazzles. As he turns his head, the gorget may appear black, then green, then flash bright red when the light reflects off it at just the right angle. Both males and females are iridescent green above. The female's underparts are white, and she sports white spots on her rounded tail. Males appear smaller and darker overall, with grayish-olive underparts and a slightly forked, all-dark tail. A squeaky chip is uttered constantly while feeding. Males sing a seldom-heard, monotonous song from exposed perches at daybreak.

WHERE DO I FIND IT? Ruby-throated hummingbirds prefer mixed deciduous woodlands with clearings, where wildflowers and abundant small insects can be found. They're fairly common in forested areas across the entire eastern United States, abruptly ending at the Great Plains. Males are conspicuous because they regularly perch on an exposed twig in between feeding sessions, watching over their territory. Virtually all rubythroats leave for the winter, many making the arduous nonstop flight across the Gulf of Mexico using energy from fat reserves. While some birds remain in the southern United States, most ruby-throats winter in Central America.

WHAT CAN I FEED OR DO TO ATTRACT IT? Blooming, nectar-producing flowers are the best way to attract hummingbirds. They are strongly attracted to red or orange flowers, but rubythroats will take nectar from flowers of any color. They hover and probe rapidly, often perching to feed. Favorite hummingbird plants include various types of bee balm, penstemon, fuchsia, jewelweed, honeysuckle, and salvia. Feeders are another good attractant. Fill hummingbird feeders with a 1:4 solution of white table sugar and water. Boiling the solution briefly helps it keep longer. Artificial coloring is unnecessary (feeders have ample red parts). Wash feeders with hot, soapy water every few days and replace the solution. To thwart a bullying male, hang several feeders within a few feet of each other. He'll be unable to defend them all. Rubythroats also take a great number of small insects, which they catch by gleaning or in aerial pursuit. They may even rob spider webs of their catch. They use spider silk in nest construction, which is a good reason to leave old spider webs in place in spring and summer on the exterior of your home— female hummingbirds are always looking for good nesting material.

NESTING Once a male rubythroat has mated, his investment in the offspring is over. The female constructs a walnut-sized, thick-walled cup of plant down and spider silk, bound tightly with elastic spider web and encrusted with lichens. This well-insulated nest protects the two pea-sized eggs when she must leave to forage. The young hatch after about 13 days and remain in the nest about 21 days. The female regurgitates small insects and nectar into their bills. Young birds are fed for at least a week after fledging.

AT A GLANCE

	–
	✔
	✔
	✔
	✔
	✔

Red-headed Woodpecker

A striking combination of red, black, and white, the red-headed wood-pecker is our most easily identifiable woodpecker and a favorite of many bird watchers. Though the species was first described in 1758, Native Americans had long used skins of the red-headed woodpecker as a battle ornament. Sadly, the red-headed has suffered population declines throughout its range, but it remains locally common in the proper habitat.

Red-headed woodpeckers are very aggressive and can outcompete European starlings for nest cavities. Look for red-heads in large stands of trees (especially oaks) with little vegetation below them, such as in a park or golf course. Reliable locations for seeing red-headed woodpeckers are becoming noteworthy as the species declines.

HOW DO I IDENTIFY IT? The red-headed woodpecker could be called the red-hooded woodpecker because the red on adult birds (both male and female) forms a complete hood. Some mistakenly refer to the red-bellied woodpecker (which has a Mohawk stripe of red) as a red-headed woodpecker. The red-head's black back and tail are set off by a bright white breast and belly and an all-white patch of secondary (inner) wing feathers. When in flight, the black-and-white flashing effect of these contrasting colors is stunning. Red-heads give a variety of *churr-churr* calls as well as a loud, throaty *queeah!*

WHERE DO I FIND IT? Prior to the 1900s, red-headed woodpeckers were a common bird in cities and towns. Today, red-heads are sparingly distributed across most of the eastern United States, usually in woods with mature oaks or beeches, in isolated woodlots along rivers, or in dead trees along flooded river bottoms and beaver ponds. Habitats affected by humans—strip mines, clear cuts, tree plantations, and farmlands—may attract red-headed woodpeckers so long as there are scattered, standing trees. These birds may nest in loose colonies with several pairs occupying a grove of trees in a good foraging habitat. If nesting is successful, these birds may return to nest year after year.

WHAT CAN I FEED OR DO TO ATTRACT IT? Red-heads have the most varied diet of all woodpeckers, but they seem especially attached to acorns and beechnuts. They are excellent flycatchers and are known to eat grasshoppers, fruits, corn, eggs, mice, and even bird nestlings. When nuts and insects are plentiful, red-heads will cache them for later consumption, hiding food items in bark crevices and knotholes. At bird feeders, red-heads eat sunflower seeds, peanuts, and suet, but they are particularly attracted to cracked corn. They will also use nest boxes for both roosting and nesting. Such housing can be made more attractive for the birds if the insides are packed with woodchips. Like other woodpeckers, red-heads prefer to do a bit of excavating before taking over a cavity. All woodpeckers enjoy using large dead trees. Placing a large tree branch or small tree trunk in your yard will enhance its appeal to woodpeckers.

NESTING Avid excavators of nesting and roosting holes, red-heads thus provide homes for many other cavity-nesting creatures. Nest holes are almost always in dead trees or dead portions of living trees, though wooden telephone poles are also used. Five eggs are the normal clutch, and both parents share in the two-week incubation duties. Young birds spend three weeks in the nest cavity before fledging, and they emerge with gray, not red, heads.

AT A GLANCE	
🏠	✔
⛲	✔
🏮	✔
🌿	✔
🎵	✔
🐦	–

Red-bellied Woodpecker

The red-bellied woodpecker is so common, vocal, and eye-catching that it might be elected "most familiar woodpecker" in a vote of bird watchers in the eastern United States. Although occasionally misidentified as a red-headed woodpecker because of the male redbelly's bill-to-nape stripe of bright red, the red-bellied woodpecker actually is quite different in appearance—and much more common—than the real red-headed woodpecker, which sports an all-red head.

HOW DO I IDENTIFY IT? A medium-sized woodpecker (9¼ inches long) with a stout, chisel-shaped bill and a zebra pattern of black-and-white horizontal strips on the back, the red-bellied woodpecker is named for a feature we rarely see—a light wash of pink or red on its belly. Hitching up tree trunks with the aid of its strong feet and stiff tail, the bird's red belly is almost always obscured. Adult males have a solid strip of red from the top of the bill and head and down the back of the neck (the nape). Females have a red nape but are brownish gray on the top of the head. In flight, the redbelly shows an obvious white rump. Like most other woodpeckers, redbellies fly in undulating swoops. The redbelly's loud, rich call sounds like *qurrr,* and its longer version is more rattling and harsher—*chrr, chrr, chrchrchrchr.*

WHERE DO I FIND IT? A year-round resident across the eastern United States, the redbelly is an adaptable bird, found wherever there are mature trees. They do not migrate, though some northern birds may move southward in winter. Red-bellied woodpeckers are common and regular visitors to backyard bird feeders and birdbaths. They are active, noisy birds and are hard not to notice wherever they are present. Some homeowners have noticed that redbellies love to do their territorial drumming (hammering their bills on a hard surface) on metal chimneys, downspouts, and aluminum siding. It seems the woodpeckers (usually males proclaiming their territories) really prefer the loud noise they can generate by hammering on metal as opposed to hammering on the wood of a tree.

WHAT CAN I FEED OR DO TO ATTRACT IT? The redbelly is an expert at excavating insects from trees using its bill as a chisel and its long, barbed tongue to extract food items. It will also eat berries, fruits, nuts, tree sap, salamanders, mice, and even small nestling birds. At bird-feeding stations, redbellies relish peanuts, suet, sunflower seeds, and cracked corn. You can also offer apple halves stuck on a tree stub, sunflower bits, mealworms, and grape jelly (in a small dish). Listen for the redbelly's loud, ringing calls and watch for its swooping flight.

NESTING The male redbelly begins courtship by drumming on a tree trunk or branch to attract the female's attention. Both male and female excavate the nest cavity, which is usually located in a dead tree below an overhanging branch. The 8- to 12-inch-deep cavity will accommodate four eggs. Incubation duties are shared and last about 12 days. Nestlings are fed in the nest cavity by both parents for almost a month before they fledge; afterward, they remain near the nest and are fed by the parents for several more weeks. Nest hole competition from European starlings can be fierce and usually results in the redbellies being evicted and forced to excavate a new nest elsewhere.

AT A GLANCE	
🏠	✔
🛁	✔
🗼	✔
🌿	–
🎵	✔
🐦	✔

Downy Woodpecker

Downy woodpeckers are a favorite of backyard bird watchers because they are often the first woodpeckers to visit bird feeders. Common in any habitat with trees, downies are equally at home in backyards and in remote woods. In all seasons, downy woodpeckers give a rattling whinny that descends in tone. They also utter a sharp pik! *call regularly while foraging. Downy woodpeckers use their stiff tails and strong, clawed feet to propel themselves along tree branches or trunks.*

HOW DO I IDENTIFY IT? The downy is the smallest (6¾ inches long), most common, and most widespread North American woodpecker. Its black-and-white plumage is similar to that of the larger (9¼ inches long) hairy woodpecker. Telling the downy and hairy woodpecker apart can be difficult. In both species, the males have a red patch at the back of the head. Downy woodpeckers have an all-white breast and belly and a white stripe down the middle of their back. The wings and tail are black with white spots. A way to remember which is which is: downy is dinky; hairy is huge. Downies have a small body, a small head, and a small, thin bill. Hairies have a big body, a big head, and a large, chisel-like bill.

WHERE DO I FIND IT? A common resident of woodlands throughout North America, the downy is a habitat generalist—found anywhere there are trees or woody plants on which to find food. Though their population appears stable, downies suffer from nest site competition from other cavity nesters and from the removal of dead trees, which they need for nesting and feeding. Look for them along the edges of woods, hitching along smaller branches, pecking and drilling for their insect-based food items. The sounds downy woodpeckers make while foraging as well as their frequent vocalizations are often the first clue to their presence.

WHAT CAN I FEED OR DO TO ATTRACT IT? Downy woodpeckers probe and chisel at a tree's bark searching for insects, insect eggs, ants, and spiders. They also eat fruits, such as sumac and poison ivy. At bird feeders, sunflower seeds, suet, peanuts, and peanut butter are favorites. They use a variety of feeder types, including hopper, tube, satellite, and suet designs. They occasionally visit hummingbird feeders for a sip of nectar. Though downies rarely nest in nest boxes, they readily use them for nighttime roosting, especially in harsh weather. If you have nest boxes for bluebirds or swallows, consider leaving them up year-round. In areas of cold winter temperatures, plug the ventilation holes with moldable weather-stripping. Leave a dead tree or large dead branch on a tree in your yard (in a safe location) and you will be much more likely to attract woodpeckers.

NESTING Like all woodpeckers, downies are cavity nesters. Each spring they excavate a new nest hole in the dead stub or trunk of a tree—usually one that is already rotting. The nest hole is placed underneath an overhanging branch higher than 12 feet above the ground. Excavation can take as long as two weeks—even with the male and female participating. Clutch size is usually four to five white eggs, which both sexes incubate. Hatching occurs at 12 days, and both parents feed the young for about three weeks until they fledge.

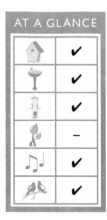

AT A GLANCE	
🏠	✔
🛁	✔
🪔	✔
🌱	–
♪	✔
🐦	✔

Hairy Woodpecker

A familiar visitor to bird feeders, the hairy woodpecker is named for the long, hairlike white feathers on its back. The hairy looks like a super-sized version of a downy woodpecker, but the best way to tell these two similar species apart is to compare the length of the bill to the length of the head (front to back). The hairy's bill is always longer than the width of its head, and the downy's bill is always shorter than the length of its head. An easier way to remember is: downy is dinky; hairy is huge.

HOW DO I IDENTIFY IT? Hairy woodpeckers are medium-sized woodpeckers (9¼ inches long) with a long, sturdy, chisel-like bill that is used for finding food, for excavating nest holes, and for territorial drumming on hollow trees. Males and females look the same, with white bellies, a white central back stripe, and distinctly patterned black and white on faces and wings. Adult males, however, have a red patch at the back of the head. Hairies utter a sharp *peek!* call, as well as a loud ringing rattle on a single pitch.

WHERE DO I FIND IT? Hairy woodpeckers are year-round residents across North America in mature forests and wherever there are large trees, including suburban backyards, urban parks, and isolated woodlots. If your neighborhood has large shade trees or mature woods, chances are good that you've got hairy woodpeckers nearby. Check large, dead snags and branches for woodpecker holes and listen for the birds' vocalizations and drumming in spring. They are one of our most widespread woodpeckers, with a range extending into Central America.

WHAT CAN I FEED OR DO TO ATTRACT IT? Using their bills, hairy woodpeckers can glean insects from tree bark or excavate them from beneath the bark's surface. Primary diet items include beetles, spiders, moth larvae, and ants, as well as fruits, seeds, and nuts. Offer peanuts, sunflower seeds, or suet (in winter) in hanging feeders to attract hairy woodpeckers to your yard. They will also be attracted to large dead trees or snags, especially if these are placed or occur naturally partway between the cover of a woodlot and your bird feeders. Hairies use these snag perches as a stopping point from which to check to see if the coast is clear before swooping in to visit your feeders.

NESTING It can take up to three weeks for a pair of hairy woodpeckers to excavate their nest cavity in the trunk or dead branch of a living tree. When completed, the nest cavity will have a 2-inch entry hole and will be 4 inches wide and as deep as 16 inches. Into this cozy space, four eggs are laid, and both parents share the roughly two-week incubation period. Less than a month after hatching, young hairies are ready to fledge from the nest, though the parents tend them for several more weeks. In spring and summer, watch for the recently fledged young woodpeckers following the adults to your feeding station, where they beg to be fed. A new nest is excavated each spring, but old cavities are used for roosting at night and in winter.

AT A GLANCE

🏠	✔
⛲	✔
🪵	✔
🌱	–
🎵	✔
🐦	✔

Northern Flicker

A familiar and fairly large woodpecker (13 inches long), the northern flicker is a distinctively marked bird that—unlike other woodpeckers—is often seen foraging on the ground. The eastern form of the flicker is known as the yellow-shafted flicker for its bright lemon-yellow underwing and tail color. A red-shafted form of the northern flicker occurs in the West. There are more than 130 different names by which the flicker is known, including high-hole, yellowhammer, and yawkerbird.

HOW DO I IDENTIFY IT? The northern flicker is all field marks with its bright yellow wing flashes, white rump, spotted breast, and barred back. It is not easily confused with any other bird. In the East, both sexes have a red crescent on the back of the head, but only males show a black "moustache" mark on the cheek. In the West, the red-shafted form of the northern flicker lacks the red crescent on the back of the head, but males show a red moustache. The flicker has several calls, including a single-note *kleer,* a short *wickawicka* series, and a monotonous *wickwickwickwick* song. It also communicates by drumming on the resonating surface of trees, poles, or even metal downspouts and chimney flues.

WHERE DO I FIND IT? The northern flicker is found almost everywhere wooded habitats exist, though open woods and woodland edges are preferred. Look for them foraging on open, grassy areas and along sidewalks, especially where there are any colonies. In their swooping, undulating flight they are hard to ignore as they flash a white rump, a brown back barred with black, and either golden-yellow or pinkish-red underwings. Flickers in the northern portion of the range migrate southward in winter, while southern birds are nonmigratory.

WHAT CAN I FEED OR DO TO ATTRACT IT? Flickers love ants. A flicker pokes its long bill into an anthill and uses its long, sticky tongue to extract the ants. They also eat other insects, as well as fruits and seeds. Offering suet, corn, sunflower seeds, grapes, or peanuts at your feeders or hung on large trees will be attractive to flickers. Providing nest boxes in your wooded backyard is another way to attract them. Equally important is the presence of ground-dwelling insects (leave those non-threatening anthills alone!) and dead trees or dead branches. A large, dead tree branch placed vertically in your yard may entice a flicker to stop and check out your other offerings.

NESTING Northern flickers excavate a new nest cavity almost every year. In doing so, they perform a much-needed service for many other hole-nesting birds—from chickadees to ducks—that use old flicker nests because they lack the strong bills and ability to excavate their own nesting cavities. Both male and female flickers excavate the nest cavity in a dead tree or branch. The female lays five to ten eggs; both sexes share the 11-day incubation period. Young flickers leave the nest after about 25 days. Flickers will use nest boxes with an interior floor of 7 × 7 inches, an interior height of 16 to 24 inches, and a 2½-inch entry hole. Because excavation is a vital part of courtship, boxes packed full of woodchips are more attractive. Competition for cavities from European starlings is fierce and may be causing a decline in flickers.

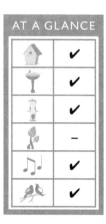

AT A GLANCE	
🏠	✔
🛁	✔
🕯	✔
🌿	–
🎵	✔
🐦	✔

Pileated Woodpecker

People who have never had a good, close look at a pileated woodpecker invariably utter an exclamation when they finally see one. This is a magnificent, flashy, loud, but shy bird—the largest living woodpecker in North America. (Recent reports of sightings of the extinct ivory-billed woodpecker remain unsubstantiated.) The word "pileated" is Latin for "capped," a reference to this woodpecker's remarkable crest. The pileated and its call, which sounds like a crazy laugh, was the inspiration for the cartoon character Woody Woodpecker.

HOW DO I IDENTIFY IT? This is a huge bird compared to our other woodpeckers. Both male and female pileated woodpeckers sport a red crest; the female's forehead is brownish and the male's is scarlet. A dull, dark charcoal-gray overall, pileateds reveal a large amount of white in the underwing when they take flight. Seen crossing high over a road, woodland clearing, or valley, their wingbeats are slow, relaxed, and steady. A closer look reveals that the wings almost seem to close between each wing beat. The call is a high, wild *yik-yik-yik-yik-yik,* suggesting a flicker, but sounding a bit wilder and not as monotonous. The pileated's hollow territorial drumming is a loud, rapid drum roll that fades away as it finishes.

WHERE DO I FIND IT? Pileateds are resident birds throughout their range. Such a large bird needs large-diameter trees. Pileated woodpeckers roost and nest in cavities that they excavate with their powerful, chisel-like bills. Older-growth forests with standing dead trees, usually in bottomland or near watercourses, are preferred by this species. In autumn, wandering pileateds may show up unexpectedly along roadsides and in yards, feasting on the fruits of sumac, firethorn, dogwood, viburnum, or other plants. Loud, chopping blows herald the presence of a feeding pileated woodpecker. These excavations sometimes sound not so much like a woodpecker as a strong person wielding an axe. Pileated woodpeckers are adaptable enough to live near humans, as long as there are large, older trees and a reliable food supply.

WHAT CAN I FEED OR DO TO ATTRACT IT? People with heavily wooded yards are sometimes successful in attracting pileated woodpeckers to raw suet or peanut butter–suet mixtures offered in sturdy cages affixed to the trunk of a large tree. Having such an impressive bird in one's yard is an event; successfully feeding one is well worth the extra effort. These birds occupy the same territories throughout their lives, so attracting one to your feeders could be the start of a long relationship. Away from feeders, pileateds often forage on rotting dead or downed trees. Palm-sized pieces of bark and punky (soft and rotted) wood fly as the bird strips bark or excavates deep, rectangular holes to reach the ant galleries and beetle larvae it needs. It is a surprisingly agile fruit plucker, clinging like an overgrown chickadee as it eats small fruits. Pileateds also glean bark and branches for insect prey.

NESTING Pileated pairs stay together year-round and presumably mate for life. Male pileated woodpeckers do most of the nest cavity excavation. The female lays four eggs, and both she and her mate incubate them; they hatch after about 16 days. Young remain in the cavity for up to 30 days, after which they have a long apprenticeship of learning to procure food with their parents.

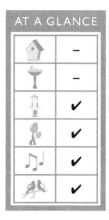

AT A GLANCE	
🏠	–
⛲	–
🪧	✔
🌿	✔
🎵	✔
🐦	✔

Eastern Phoebe

A very adaptable, sparrow-sized flycatcher, the eastern phoebe often nests on building ledges, inside barns, under bridges, and in culverts. Nesting in such proximity to humans, phoebes are used to our activity and this apparent tameness allows us to think of them as "our phoebes." Many bird watchers consider the early spring return of the eastern phoebe (not the American robin) to be the most reliable sign of spring. The eastern phoebe is a perch-and-wait hunter, watching for flying insects from an exposed perch and making short flying forays to nab its prey. Phoebes consume vast quantities of flying insects but will also pluck food from the ground or vegetation. Wasps, bees, flying ants, moths, and butterflies constitute much of their prey. In fall and winter, when insects are scarce, phoebes switch their diet to small fruits and berries.

HOW DO I IDENTIFY IT?   The eastern phoebe, unlike most other drab-colored flycatchers that may be conused with one another, is relatively easy to identify. A medium-sized bird that constantly wags its tail, the phoebe also gives a vocal clue to its identity by softly uttering its name—*fee-bee . . . fee-bee*. Eastern phoebes are a dark, drab gray-brown on the back, with faint wing bars and a light breast and belly, often washed with yellow. Many of our other, less common flycatchers show an obvious white eye ring, which the eastern phoebe lacks.

WHERE DO I FIND IT?   Wherever there is a suitable nesting ledge (with abundant flying insects nearby), phoebes may be found. During the nesting season, look for them near bridges and culverts over streams, inside old barns and abandoned farm houses, and even under the eaves and decks of suburban homes. Natural habitats include woodland edges and clearings, roadsides, parks, and rocky outcroppings along small streams. Phoebes are often heard calling before they are seen. Or they may catch your eye by darting out from a perch to catch an insect, then swooping back to that same perch to eat their catch. Common throughout most of eastern North America during spring and summer, in winter many phoebes migrate to the southern Atlantic Coast and the Gulf Coast into Mexico.

WHAT CAN I FEED OR DO TO ATTRACT IT?   Bird watchers love phoebes not only because they are common, but also because they are so full of energy and seem willing to make their nests in close proximity to humans. To attract phoebes to your property, place nesting shelves (about 6 × 8 inches) about a foot below the eaves of your house, garage, or outbuilding. Choose a site away from human activity that is as safe as possible from predators, such as snakes, raccoons, and cats. Enhancing your landscape with fruit- and berry-producing plants can give phoebes and other birds a source of food in cold weather when insects are not active.

NESTING   Phoebes are early nesters and often begin almost immediately after a male attracts a mate to a likely site. Favored natural nest sites include rock ledges and caves, but they also nest in barns or outbuildings and on handy ledges or sills on house porches. The female builds the cup-shaped nest out of mud, moss, and grass. Four to six eggs are laid and incubated by the female alone, for just over two weeks. Young phoebes, unless disturbed earlier, fledge after about 16 days.

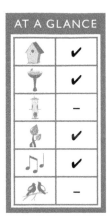

AT A GLANCE

🏠	✔
⛲	✔
🏮	–
🌿	✔
♪	✔
🐦	–

Blue Jay

Blue jays are smart, adaptable, noisy birds. They often mimic the call of a red-tailed or red-shouldered hawk as they approach your bird feeder in an apparent attempt to scare other birds away. Sometimes persecuted by humans as nest-robbers or bullies at the feeding station, blue jays are one of our most ornate and lovely birds. Blue jays are no friend to hawks and owls and will often alert other birds to their presence. When a number of jays collect to pester a raptor, this behavior is called mobbing.

HOW DO I IDENTIFY IT?   No other eastern bird is blue and crested, making the blue jay unmistakable. They are large, measuring 11 inches from bill tip to tail end. Males and females are similar, showing a black necklace that separates a white face and throat from a gray chest. The back is various shades of blue with obvious white spots in the blue wings and on the tips of the tail feathers. Besides the standard *jay jay* or *jeer jeer* call often used as a scold, blue jays emit a variety of squeaks, rattles, and croaks in addition to mimicking other birds' calls. If you hear a sound in the woods that is loud and unmusical, chances are good that it's a blue jay. Blue jays fly in a straight line with a rowing motion of the wings. As they fly from one patch of woods to another across an opening, they often turn their head from side to side, wary of a possible attack from a marauding hawk.

WHERE DO I FIND IT?   Look for blue jays along woodland edges and listen for their raucous cries, almost always the first clue to their presence. Blue jays prefer woods with oaks and beeches. The blue jay has a special relationship with oaks, burying as many as five thousand acorns in individual spots in fall (called caches). Many of these acorns are never retrieved, so jays are credited with helping regenerate and diversify our forests. Resident throughout their range, especially in the deep South, blue jays in northern latitudes migrate southward in early fall, traveling by daylight in flocks of ten or more, many carrying acorns in their bills.

WHAT CAN I FEED OR DO TO ATTRACT IT?   Blue jays eat almost anything. Grasshoppers and other insects, and acorns and other nuts, are their primary foods. Bird eggs or nestlings, mice, frogs, and a variety of human-supplied foods are also eaten. When storing acorns, blue jays will carry as many as five acorns in their throat and bill to the cache site, drop them in a pile, and bury them one at a time. A common feeder visitor, blue jays like suet, peanuts, sunflower seeds, cracked corn, and even dog food. A source of water is highly attractive to blue jays, so keep the birdbath clean and filled.

AT A GLANCE

🏠	–
🚰	✔
🪆	✔
🌿	✔
🎵	✔
🐦	–

NESTING   Males help gather nesting materials, but females do most of the building in a tree. The twig nest is woven into a cup and lined with wet leaves and rootlets. Suburban blue jays often incorporate string, plastics, paper, and other human trash into their nest. The female lays four to six eggs and incubates them for 18 days, followed by about 20 days of care before the young jays fledge.

American Crow

The American crow is our most widespread and common member of the corvid family, which includes crows, ravens, jays, and magpies. Noisy, sly, opportunistic, and ubiquitous, the American crow lives among us, yet comparatively little is known about it. Like other bold, brash members of the corvid family (the blue jay being a prime example), the crow is downright sneaky where its personal life is concerned. Few people know that crows may breed cooperatively in groups of up to a dozen birds, helping tend the dominant pair's nest. Loud, bordering on obnoxious, most of the year, crows are incredibly quiet during nesting.

HOW DO I IDENTIFY IT? American crows are glossy black from bill to toenail. They are armed with a stout, strong bill that acts as a chisel, axe, shovel, or forceps, among other uses. The crow's distinctive wing beats appear to row the bird through the sky. Crows are well known for their raucous caw. Evidence from field studies suggests that crows have different "words" for different situations (flock assembly, dispersal, mobbing); their language is complex, as is their social behavior. Few are privileged to hear the crow's song, given by both sexes, which is a long recitation of rattles, coos, growls, and imitations of sounds. The common raven is a larger, stockier relative of the American crow. In flight, ravens show a wedge-shaped tail—crows show a square-ended tail. Ravens are as common as crows in parts of the West, in the far North, and in the eastern mountains. In the coastal Southeast the smaller, more nasal-sounding fish crow can be confused with the American crow.

WHERE DO I FIND IT? Though they are strongly associated with farmland and open areas with scattered woodlots, crows find perfect conditions in cities and suburbs, where they raid pet dishes, bird feeders, and garbage cans. In the northern part of their range, crows are migratory, but all American crows spend the winter within the continental United States. Throughout their range, when not breeding, crows gather into large roosts, and these can swell to thousands of birds by late winter.

WHAT CAN I FEED OR DO TO ATTRACT IT? Crows are always up to something, and feeding them gives us an opportunity to observe their always-intriguing behavior. To find something a crow might like, open the refrigerator. Freezer-burned meat is a favorite. Cracked or whole corn is irresistible as well. Neighbors may wonder, but crows are well worth watching. There's almost nothing edible an American crow will not eat. At roadkills, landfills, and compost piles, crows will load their distensible throat with food and fly heavily off, often caching it under leaves or sod for later enjoyment. Crows forage by walking slowly on the ground—hunting invertebrates and vertebrates alike—and are constantly scanning roadsides and fields as they fly, descending to investigate anything that might be edible.

NESTING Crows stay in family units composed of parents and their young from the previous year. These yearlings may help build the nest, incubate, or feed the incubating female or her young. Four or five eggs are laid in the bulky twig nest, which is usually hidden high in a pine. The female incubates for around 17 days, and young fledge at around 36 days. Their strangled, nasal calls sometimes betray the nest location.

AT A GLANCE	
🏠	–
🍽	✔
🏮	✔
🌾	–
🎵	✔
🐦	–

Purple Martin

No other North American bird has a closer association with humans than the purple martin. For more than four hundred years, martins in eastern North America have nested in human-supplied housing, at first in hollow gourds offered by Native Americans and today in a variety of specialized houses designed just for them. Even non–bird watchers appreciate this friendly and familiar bird. Purple martins eat flying insects almost exclusively, but—contrary to popular opinion and marketing hype—do not eat many mosquitoes. Mosquitoes, after all, are small, nocturnal insects. Martins forage by day, flying over open fields and bodies of water swooping after larger airborne insects, such as beetles, flies, dragonflies, wasps, butterflies, and moths.

HOW DO I IDENTIFY IT? Our largest swallow (at 8 inches), the purple martin is a graceful flyer with a bubbly, liquid song. The adult male has a deep blue body and black wings and tail. His iridescent plumage has a sheen that, in bright sunlight, may show some of the purplish tones that give the species its name. Female and young purple martins are gray and black with some blue on the back. In flight, martins can be confused with European starlings—both have triangular wings—but martins have a notched tail and call out almost constantly.

WHERE DO I FIND IT? Purple martins breed across eastern North America, except for in the extreme North. Because they rely on human-supplied housing, most martins are found around cities and towns. Purple martins nest in colonies; in the East, these colonies are made up of housing placed in an appropriate habitat. In the West, purple martins use old woodpecker cavities for nesting in trees, power poles, and even large cacti in the Southwest. Martin colonies are noisy, active things with birds constantly coming and going, calling, and fighting as they sort out nesting sites and tend to eggs or young. Purple martins spend the spring and summer in North America. They spend winters in South America but return to the southern United States in mid-January, their arrival eagerly anticipated.

WHAT CAN I FEED OR DO TO ATTRACT IT? Martins are rather selective in choosing colony nest sites, but they like to be with other martins. Research reveals they prefer white housing with a large interior (8 × 8 × 8 inches) and a 1½-inch entry hole. The housing should be mounted near a human dwelling in an open area. Your chances of attracting martins are greater if there is an existing colony within a mile. Nearby water ensures a steady supply of insects for hungry martins. The most successful martin landlords are those willing to care for their tenants with predator-proof housing, elimination of competing house sparrows and starlings, and regular monitoring. In cold, rainy weather, martin landlords often feed them mealworms and bits of scrambled egg in an effort to keep their beloved birds alive. Some even shoot mealworms into the air with a plastic spoon just so the martins can catch their food in flight.

NESTING Martins build a loose cup nest inside a cavity out of pine needles and grass, lined with green leaves (which limit parasites). The female lays four to six eggs and does most of the incubation, lasting about 16 days. Both parents feed the nestlings for the month-long period before fledging.

AT A GLANCE	
🏠	✔
⛲	–
🏮	–
🥄	–
♫	✔
🐦	✔

Tree Swallow

The lovely tree swallow is expanding its breeding range into the southern United States. Elsewhere, it's established and common in spring and summer (with the exception of the most arid regions and habitats). Previously limited by the availability of their required nesting cavities, tree swallows benefit greatly from artificial nest boxes erected to attract eastern bluebirds. Their liquid twittering, sharp blue-and-white color, and trusting ways make them welcome in your backyard. Before the advent of artificial nest boxes, tree swallows nested in old woodpecker holes—a hotly contested resource. Scores of birds, other animals, and even bees and wasps may be contending for a limited number of old woodpecker holes.

HOW DO I IDENTIFY IT?   Long, triangular wings, snowy white under-parts, and glossy teal blue upperparts make the tree swallow a beautiful signal of spring. Soaring kitelike, then rising with rapid flaps, they course and dive over meadows and ponds in their search for flying insects. Their jingling calls have been likened to the sound of someone shaking paperclips in a tumbler. Females are somewhat browner above and a duller blue than males. Juvenile birds are brown-backed and white below.

WHERE DO I FIND IT?   Tree swallows prefer open fields, preferably near water, for nesting, though they will inhabit upland sites. Marshes—fresh and salt—provide the flying insects they require. The tree swallow's breeding habitat extends across Canada and the northern tier of the United States and is rapidly expanding into the Southeast. Tree swallows winter in coastal areas from South Carolina to Florida and along the Gulf Coast into Mexico and Central America. They are found year-round in much of central and southern California. In late summer, tree swallows gather in large pre-migratory flocks sometimes numbering thousands. They migrate in small flocks, with many birds heading as far south as Central America. Others remain in the coastal United States, eating fruits when cold weather kills flying insects.

WHAT CAN I FEED OR DO TO ATTRACT IT?   Eighty percent of its diet is insects; fruits make up the rest, mainly bayberries that sustain it in adverse winter weather. This ability to eat fruit helps tree swallows survive cold snaps as they make their way northward to breed. Insects are caught on the wing in spectacular zigzag flights and are stored in the throat to be fed to nestlings. Allowing your property to naturally produce flying insects will attract tree swallows. The very best way to attract them is to erect nest boxes with a 1⁹⁄₁₆-inch hole, mounted on a predator-proof pole in an open meadow near water; it's virtually guaranteed to catch the attention of a passing tree swallow. Get the housing up early in spring, since tree swallows are often the first of our swallows to return.

NESTING   A foundation of coarse grass, leaves, and stems is lined with large body feathers, usually white. Tree swallows are mad for feathers in nesting season and can often be induced to take soft white feathers from your hand. A New York study showed that eggs hatched and nestlings survived better in nests insulated with more feathers. The female incubates four to seven eggs for an average of 14 days. Young leave the nest 15 to 25 days later, flying strongly. Second broods are rare, but seem to be more frequent in the South.

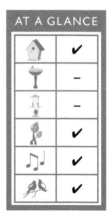

AT A GLANCE	
🏠	✔
(bird bath)	–
(feeder)	–
🌿	✔
🎵	✔
🐦	✔

Barn Swallow

The barn swallow is named for its preferred nesting location of barns. This species seems to define what it means to be at home in the air. One early naturalist estimated that a barn swallow that lived ten years would fly more than two million miles, enough to travel eighty-seven times around the earth. One of the most familiar and beloved birds in rural America, the barn swallow is welcomed everywhere as a sign of spring. Nothing says "country" more than a pair of barn swallows zipping in and out of the open doors of a working barn, darting after insects and chattering incessantly. Sometimes two or three pairs will share a favored site during nesting season. They ignore the normal activity of the people and animals that regularly use the barn, but if a strange person or animal approaches, the adults will swoop and chatter and snap their bills at the trespasser.

HOW DO I IDENTIFY IT?   Glossy blue-black above and orange below, the barn swallow is the only American swallow that has a true "swallow tail," with an elongated outer pair of tail feathers forming a deep V. The females are not quite as glossy or highly colored, and the fork in their tails is not quite as pronounced. Like all swallows, they have short legs and rather weak feet used for perching, not walking. They are much more graceful in flight than on the ground. The similar-looking cliff swallow prefers to nest on rocky cliffs and under bridges, as its name suggests. It is not as common around human habitation as is the barn swallow. The cliff swallow shows a pale tan forehead and rump and lacks the barn swallow's deeply notched tail.

WHERE DO I FIND IT?   The barn swallow may be found over any open area, such as pastures, fields, and golf courses, as well as lakes, ponds, and rivers. It has adapted well to humans and is not shy of people, nesting close to settled areas as long as it has open space for feeding. Barn swallows travel in great flocks during migrations, often in company with other swallow species. They arrive in most of their U.S. range in April and leave in early to mid-fall.

WHAT CAN I FEED OR DO TO ATTRACT IT?   Foraging almost entirely on the wing, the barn swallow takes a variety of insect prey, from flies and locusts to moths, grasshoppers, bees, and wasps. Occasionally small berries or seeds are eaten, but this is uncommon. Only in bad weather will barn swallows feed on the ground. During breeding season, you may bring barn swallows into close range by throwing white feathers into the air near a flock of soaring birds; the graceful fliers will swoop in to snatch them up to use for nest linings. Barn swallows also enjoy eating bits of baked eggshells during breeding season. Bake the shells at 250° Fahrenheit for 20 minutes to sterilize them, then crumble into small bits and sprinkle on the ground.

NESTING   The barn swallow's nest is a cup of mud and grass, lined with feathers and placed on a rafter or glued under an eave. Besides barns, other open buildings, covered porches, or the undersides of bridges or docks are used. During second nestings, immatures from the first brood help feed and care for their younger siblings.

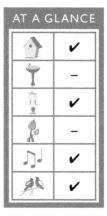

AT A GLANCE

🏠	✔
🏺	–
🔦	✔
🌿	–
🎵	✔
🐦	✔

Carolina & Black-capped Chickadee

Gregarious and widespread, chickadees are just about everyone's favorite backyard birds. In the southern United States, the resident chickadee is actually the Carolina chickadee, a slightly smaller but otherwise quite similar cousin of the black-capped chickadee of the northern half of the United States. Chickadees travel in noisy little bands and draw attention to themselves with their frequent scolding chatter. In winter, their flock-mates may include titmice, nuthatches, wrens, creepers, kinglets, and other species. Chickadees are often the first birds to discover a newly installed bird feeder.

HOW DO I IDENTIFY IT? Both chickadees have black caps and bibs as well as white cheek patches; gray backs, wings, and tails; and pale underparts with buff-colored flanks. Males and females are alike, and there are no seasonal differences in plumage. In general, black-capped chickadees are larger (5¼ inches long) and bigger-headed, with brighter white cheeks. Carolina chickadees are drabber gray overall, are smaller (4¾ inches long), and have less white in the wings. Vocal clues can be helpful. Black-cappeds sing *fee-bee* (two notes) while Carolinas sing *soo-fee, soo-fay* (four notes). The common *chick-a-dee-dee-dee* call is lower, hoarser, and slower from black-cappeds, and higher and more melodic from Carolinas.

WHERE DO I FIND IT? Black-capped chickadees prefer open deciduous woods with oaks, willows, birches, and alders among their favored trees. This species is resident (nonmigratory) and throughout most of its range it is the only chickadee present. It is generally replaced by the Carolina chickadee in the southern half of the eastern states. The dividing line between the ranges of our two widespread chickadee species runs from central New Jersey west through Pennsylvania, Ohio, Indiana, Illinois, Missouri, Kansas, Oklahoma, and Texas. North of this line it's mostly black-capped chickadees; south of it, primarily Carolina chickadees. Where the two species overlap they may occasionally interbreed, so identifying individual birds under such circumstances is tricky. Black-cappeds will occasionally move south in winter.

WHAT CAN I FEED OR DO TO ATTRACT IT? Chickadees have a varied diet. Nearly half of the food taken in the wild consists of insects. They also eat spiders, weed seeds, and the seeds and small fruits of many trees (maples, oaks, birches) and vines like grapes, Virginia creeper, and honeysuckle. It is easy to lure chickadees into your yard by providing black-oil sunflower seed in hanging tubes or hopper feeders and by offering suet or other fats, such as a peanut butter–cornmeal mix or "bird pudding." They also enjoy peanuts, mealworms, and a reliable source of clean water. To induce a pair to stay and nest, install one or more nest boxes with entrance holes that are 1¼ to 1½ inches in diameter.

NESTING Cavity nesters, chickadees seek out natural holes in woodland trees, often adapting old woodpecker holes. They readily accept not only nesting boxes but also crevices under eaves or porch roofs, hollowe-out fence posts, or drainpipes. The nest is a thick mass of mosses, bark, and grasses, enclosing a cup of soft hair. One side is built up higher than the other and can be pulled down like a flap to cover the young when both parents are away. As many as eight eggs are laid and incubated by the female for 11 to 13 days; both parents then share the feeding of the young until they fledge after two weeks.

AT A GLANCE

🏠	✔
⚱	✔
🪔	✔
🌿	✔
♫	✔
🐦	–

Tufted Titmouse

The "mouse" portion of the tufted titmouse's name probably comes from its beady black eyes, which stand out against a plain, pale face. From deep mixed woods to old orchards, from city parks to leafy suburban backyards, this friendly and active little bird makes itself at home year-round. It's noisy and sociable, quite tame around humans, and fearless among other small birds with which it associates. Its cheerful calls of peter, peter, peter *ring out even in midwinter. In winter tufted titmice travel in mixed flocks with chickadees, sparrows, woodpeckers, and kinglets. Tufted titmice are easy to locate by their noisy, scolding calls. When they sound especially agitated it's a good bet that they've located a predator, such as an owl, hawk, snake, cat, or fox. Along with their close chickadee relatives, titmice are the watchdogs of the woodlot and backyard, alerting other birds to danger.*

HOW DO I IDENTIFY IT?   The tufted titmouse is 6¼ inches long and dressed primly across its upperparts in gray, with a creamy breast and rusty flanks. A black button-eye stands out and a crest adorns its head. Its small, sharp bill is black, as are its legs and feet. Titmice are very vocal and, besides their signature calls, they have a variety of whistled notes—similar to the northern cardinal and Carolina wren. Their harsh, raspy, scolding notes are similar to the chickadee's.

WHERE DO I FIND IT?   The tufted titmouse was originally considered a southern woodland bird, but for the past 50 years it has been expanding its range northward and westward. The species' affinity for bird feeders and nesting boxes has played a part, as has the regeneration of wooded habitat. Titmice are nonmigratory and able to survive harsh weather as long as sufficient food is available.

WHAT CAN I FEED OR DO TO ATTRACT IT?   Tufted titmice eat mostly insects and seeds, depending on time of year. Caterpillars are popular in summer, but they also take wasps and bees, scale insects, beetles, the larvae of many species, and, in winter, insect eggs. Acorns are a mainstay in fall and winter. At feeders, titmice relish sunflower seeds, suet, suet dough, and peanuts. They often snag a single seed and fly away to crack it open to consume the nutmeat inside. The natural nesting choice of the tufted titmouse is a tree cavity—an abandoned woodpecker hole, or a crack caused by a lightning strike. Other sites include rotted fence posts and drainage pipes. Tufted titmice will breed in nest boxes, especially those with an entrance hole in the 1½-inch diameter range. Boxes placed along woodland edges or inside the woods are most likely to be used for nesting or roosting by the tufted titmouse.

AT A GLANCE

NESTING   The female builds the nest of grass, moss, bark, and leaves, filling up whatever spot they have adopted. When the main structure is completed, the birds line it with hair, often plucked from a living animal—woodchuck, rabbit, dog, or even a handy human. Five or six eggs are laid, incubated by the female for 12 to 14 days. Both parents feed the young, which fledge at about 15 days. The family group stays together, sometimes into the next year, and year-old birds may help their parents care for the nestlings of the newest brood.

White-breasted Nuthatch

The word "nuthatch" refers to their habit of wedging a seed in a crevice and then hacking or "hatching" it open by pounding at it with their chisel-like bill. Nuthatches are often referred to as "upside-down birds" because they forage by probing tree trunks with their heads facing downward. During their journeys down the trunk of a tree, they often pause, and then raise their head so that it is parallel to the ground—a unique posture among birds. The best-known family member is the white-breasted nuthatch, a bird of deciduous woods and tree-filled backyards. In woodlands, listen for the nuthatch's nasal honking calls anytime. Males and females always forage near each other and, in winter, in a mixed flock with chickadees and titmice.

HOW DO I IDENTIFY IT? At nearly 6 inches, the white-breasted nuthatch is the largest nuthatch. Males have gray backs with black caps, white underparts, and a beady black eye on a white face. Females are similar but wear gray on their heads. White-breasteds are thick-necked and short-tailed, with a stocky appearance. White-breasted nuthatch calls—uttered frequently in all seasons—are a nasal and repetitive *ank-ank*. If you see a medium-sized gray, black, and white bird, scooting down a tree trunk, stopping to probe with its bill, chances are you're watching a white-breasted nuthatch. Its cousins, the red-breasted of the far North and West, the brown-headed of the Southeast, and the pygmy of the western mountains, are all much smaller and less conspicuous.

WHERE DO I FIND IT? White-breasted nuthatches prefer older deciduous woods, but are found in large parks and leafy backyards. They are active birds, calling regularly and almost constantly moving, whether foraging in a natural woodland setting or at a backyard feeding station. In northern coniferous woods, and at high elevations along the Appalachian chain, they are replaced by the smaller red-breasted nuthatch, while the brown-headed nuthatch displaces them in the dry pinewoods of the South. In the West, the pygmy nuthatch occurs in pine woods of the mountains.

WHAT CAN I FEED OR DO TO ATTRACT IT? The white-breasted nuthatch eats both insects and seeds, varying its fare with the seasons. Insects make up nearly 100 percent of their summer diet, with seeds being added in fall and winter. Autumn's extra seeds and nuts are sometimes stashed in tree bark crevices to be eaten later. White-breasted nuthatches will come to feeders for black-oil sunflower and other seeds, peanuts, or suet, but they tend to abandon backyard feeders almost entirely in spring and summer when insects are plentiful. Nuthatches are cavity nesters, but they seem to prefer tree cavities to nest boxes. Leaving old, dead trees standing—where this can be done safely—offers nuthatches potential foraging, "hatching," and nesting sites.

AT A GLANCE

	✔
	✔
	✔
	–
	✔
	✔

NESTING Nuthatches maintain their pair bond and territory all year. The nest is placed in a natural cavity, old woodpecker hole, or, more rarely, a nest box. Built by the female, it is a cup of grasses, bark strips, and twigs lined with hair. When the nest is finished, the nuthatches "sweep" the entrance with their bills, rubbing a crushed insect against the wood—the chemicals released may repel predators. The female incubates a clutch of eight eggs for two weeks. Both parents feed the young for at least two weeks until fledging.

Red-breasted Nuthatch

Creeping along pine branches like a tiny mechanical toy, the red-breasted nuthatch is looking for seeds and for insects, spiders, and other edible morsels. Its small size and preference for northern coniferous forests may make it a less familiar sight to many backyard bird watchers. However, when the natural food crop is poor in the red-breasted nuthatches' year-round range in the North and the mountain areas of the East and West, these birds will venture south and to lower elevations in search of food. During these "invasion" years, red-breasted nuthatches can become familiar visitors at backyard feeding stations. Like other nuthatches, the red-breasted forages on trees by working its way from the top downward, often going all the way to the ground along the trunk before flying off to the high branches of another tree. Strong, long-toed feet with sharp claws help the nuthatch to maintain a grip on the tree bark, even when hanging upside-down.

HOW DO I IDENTIFY IT? This small nuthatch (4½ inches long) is not really red on its breast—it's more orange or rusty. Another key field mark is the bold black line through the eye, which both males and females show, though males are more richly colorful. This eyeline, the smaller size, and the male's rich rusty breast and belly help tell this nuthatch apart from the larger, more common white-breasted nuthatch. Male red-breasted nuthatches are black-headed and gray-backed, while females are gray-headed and gray-backed. The call of the red-breasted nuthatch is a series of high-pitched nasal toots, which some bird watchers say sounds like a tiny tin horn. It also gives a rapid series of toots and squeaks when excited.

WHERE DO I FIND IT? Though they will visit all kinds of trees, especially in winter, red-breasted nuthatches seem to prefer conifers of all types during most of the year, including during the breeding season. They are year-round residents in the northern forests from the Canadian Maritimes and New England to the mountain forests of the West as far as Alaska. In winter, they can be found almost anywhere in the continental United States except for the Florida peninsula and South Texas. Any large stand of pines is worth checking in winter for red-breasted nuthatches.

WHAT CAN I FEED OR DO TO ATTRACT IT? Planting conifers like pines, spruces, hemlocks, or firs will put out the welcome mat for these birds, though you may have to be patient until the trees grow large enough to produce the cones from which the nuthatches get seeds. They will also visit bird feeders, particularly for sunflower seeds and hearts, peanuts, suet, and suet dough. Their ability to cling makes it easy for them to visit any type of feeder. And it's always a good idea to have a well-maintained birdbath, since most of our backyard birds need water for drinking and bathing.

NESTING A mated pair will share the work of excavating a nesting cavity, then the female prepares the nest inside it using fine grasses, rootlets, and moss. They often spread sticky pine sap (or "pitch") around the nest cavity entrance to discourage other birds and creatures from entering. Four or more eggs are laid and incubated by the female for 12 days. The male feeds the female during incubation and both parents feed the nestlings until fledging day about three weeks later.

Carolina Wren

Creeping and exploring around stoops, garages, house eaves, and tool sheds, Carolina wrens adopt a mi casa es su casa *policy when it comes to nesting. If you find a nest cleverly hidden on a cluttered shelf or in a hanging flower basket, it's likely that of a Carolina wren. Their persistent songs, often given as a duet between a mated pair, brighten winter days and ring through the thick underbrush that they prefer. Carolina wrens are so curious and bold that they have been known to enter houses through open doors and windows to seek food. Highly intelligent, they easily find their way back outside and make charming neighbors. Listen for their ringing whistles in any low-lying tangled woods, and enjoy them in your yard.*

HOW DO I IDENTIFY IT? The Carolina wren is a rotund, warm-brown bird that often carries its tail cocked upward. Leading with its longish, curved bill, it resembles a little brown teapot. Reinforcing this impression is the phrase it often sings: *teakettle, teakettle teakettle, teakettle!* The bright white line over its eye and its warm buffy underparts (paler in summer) help clinch the identification. Males and females look alike.

WHERE DO I FIND IT? Carolina wrens are common from southern New England to Florida and to the eastern edge of the Great Plains. They have slowly expanded their range to the north, helped in part by bird-feeding stations. The Carolina wren stays as a year-round resident. It's most common in swampy, mixed hardwood forests that are thick with vines, shrubs, and tangles, but it's happy in yards and gardens with plenty of shrubbery, brush piles, and outbuildings. Carolina wrens love poking about stacks of firewood, and they'll help themselves to the shelter of an open porch, garage, or shed, cleverly concealing their nests in and amongst our clutter.

WHAT CAN I FEED OR DO TO ATTRACT IT? Insects and spiders make up virtually all the Carolina wren's natural diet. At times, they will climb trees to glean insects hidden in bark or toss aside leaf litter while searching for prey. They'll bash large prey, such as katydids and moths, into manageable pieces and hunt cobwebby corners for spiders. In snowy winters, Carolina wrens can become regular visitors at your feeding station. Though they're unable to crack seeds with their fine, curved bills, Carolina wrens poke about for fragments of sunflower hearts and swallow white millet whole. They're most fond of peanuts, peanut butter–suet mixtures, and mealworms. Perhaps the best way to attract Carolina wrens is to hang an old coffee can in the corner of an outbuilding, open garage, carport, or porch. While they will sometimes use nest boxes, Carolina wrens have an almost perverse preference for odd nesting sites like clothespin bags, old shoes, and nail cans in tool sheds.

NESTING Carolina wrens weave a surprisingly complex and bulky nest, hauling volumes of bark strips, fine twigs, leaves, grasses, green moss, and rubbish into a hidden nook, thick intertwining of vines, natural tree cavity, or cranny in an outbuilding. They often make a "porch" of such material leading to the nest. The entire affair is domed, and the finely woven inner cup holds four eggs. The female incubates for 14 days while the male feeds her. The young leave the nest 12 to 19 days later.

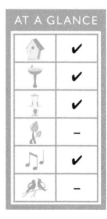

AT A GLANCE	
🏠	✔
⛲	✔
🕯	✔
🌿	–
🎵	✔
🐦	–

House Wren

The rich and burbling song of the house wren is surprisingly loud for such a tiny bird (4¾ inches long). House wrens are named for their preference for living in close proximity to humans, often in tiny wren houses that we provide for them. This mostly plain brown bird makes up for its small size and drab color by being a fierce competitor for nesting sites. In fact, backyard landlords who wish to provide housing for bluebirds, swallows, and purple martins sometimes learn the hard way that it's best to place their housing away from the edge of the woods where territorial house wrens may take them over and evict the intended tenants. The house wren's song and scolding calls are heard often wherever they are present.

HOW DO I IDENTIFY IT? House wrens are notable for their lack of field marks. Their warm-brown upperparts and tail are matched by a grayish breast. Look closely at the house wren and you'll see a variety of small white and black spots, the only variation in the bird's subtly beautiful plumage. Males and females look alike and both have the habit, characteristic of wrens, of cocking their tails up when perched. The thin, slightly curved bill is ideal for capturing and eating the house wren's insect prey. As they forage in thick cover near the ground, with their small size and brown coloration, house wrens can look a lot like tiny, feathered mice.

WHERE DO I FIND IT? Spending the summers in thickets and brushy edge habitat adjacent to woodlands, the house wren is a familiar bird in parks, backyards, and gardens, often—but not always—near human settlements. They are most often heard singing their long, rich, burbling song before they are seen. Some house wrens winter in the southernmost states in the United States, but many travel beyond our borders farther south.

WHAT CAN I FEED OR DO TO ATTRACT IT? Insects and arachnids make up the house wren's diet (grasshoppers, crickets, spiders, and moths are on the menu), but they will also eat snails and caterpillars. Most of their foraging is done in thick vegetation on or near the ground. Wren houses are the best way to attract them. House wrens will readily accept nest boxes with interior dimensions of 4 × 4 inches and entry holes of 1¼ inches in diameter. Nest boxes placed adjacent to brushy habitat or a wood's edge seem to be the most attractive. Nest boxes for bluebirds and tree swallows should be placed far from edge habitat, in the open, to avoid conflict and competition from territorial house wrens.

NESTING House wrens nest in a variety of locations, from woodpecker holes to natural cavities and nest boxes. Like Carolina wrens, house wrens will also nest in flowerpots, drainpipes, and other such sites. They are very competitive about nesting sites, often filling all or most available cavities with sticks. The male builds these "dummy" nests, and the female selects one in which to nest. The twig structures are lined with soft materials, such as grass or hair, and the female lays six to eight eggs. She performs the incubation duties, which last from 12 to 14 days. Fledglings leave the nest two or more weeks after hatching. House wrens are known to pierce the eggs of other cavity-nesting birds in their territories.

AT A GLANCE

house	✔
bath	✔
feeder	–
plant	–
song	✔
pair	–

Eastern Bluebird

The eastern bluebird is our most famous thrush, even more popular than its cousin, the American robin. Its beauty, song, and willingness to live close to us has inspired poets, songwriters, artists, and bird watchers. You can attract bluebirds to your yard if you have a large, open lawn, especially if you provide housing. Thanks to a concerted effort by bluebird lovers to provide nest boxes, the eastern bluebird has rebounded from its low population in the 1960s. Bluebirds catch insects on the ground in grassy areas, so they are particularly vulnerable to lawn chemicals.

HOW DO I IDENTIFY IT? The sky-blue back and rusty breast of the male eastern bluebird are echoed in the female's more muted tones. There are three bluebird species in North America, but only the eastern is commonly found in the eastern half of the continent. Eastern bluebirds are often seen perched along fence lines, on wires, or high in trees. They may appear all dark in bright sunlight, so many miss seeing them. When perched, eastern bluebirds look round-bodied and round-headed. During spring courtship, paired bluebirds can be seen fluttering their wings near a prospective nesting site, uttering their rich *turalee turalay* song.

WHERE DO I FIND IT? Eastern bluebirds are resident throughout the eastern United States in open habitats, such as pastures, grasslands, parks, and large suburban lawns (especially where bluebird nest boxes are available). The two habitat requirements of bluebirds are large, open, grassy areas for foraging and cavities for roosting and nesting. In harsh winter weather, bluebirds may migrate short distances to find food or shelter. Winter flocks, mostly adults and offspring from the previous breeding season, may stay in wooded habitat during harsh weather. On sunny winter days they will emerge to hunt for insects.

WHAT CAN I FEED OR DO TO ATTRACT IT? From an elevated perch, bluebirds watch for moving insects and then drop to the ground to pounce on them or to capture them in midair. They eat insects year-round and will shift to fruits and berries when insects are scarce. If you have a large expanse of open, grassy habitat, place a snag or two in the middle of it for bluebirds to use for foraging. If you offer houses, place them (with 1½-inch entrance holes) on metal poles with a pole-mounted baffle beneath the house to prevent predators from raiding the nests. House locations should be in the middle of a large, open, grassy lawn or field. It's important to monitor and manage your bluebird houses to keep house sparrows and starlings from usurping them and to keep predators from eating the eggs or young. Bluebirds visit feeders for mealworms, berries, and suet or suet dough.

NESTING Bluebirds are cavity nesters and will use old woodpecker holes or natural cavities in trees. Human-supplied nest boxes are important sites. The female bluebird builds the nest inside the cavity using bark strips, grass, and hair. She lays four to six eggs and incubates them for 12 to 16 days. Both parents care for the nestlings until fledging occurs after 14 to 18 days. If bluebirds are successful with an early spring or summer nesting, they will nest again using the same location. If they are unsuccessful, they will usually move to another location before attempting to nest again.

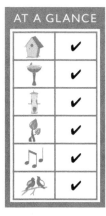

AT A GLANCE

🏠	✔
⛲	✔
🪔	✔
🌿	✔
🎵	✔
🐦	✔

Wood Thrush

The haunting, flutelike song of the wood thrush inspires bird watchers, naturalists, poets, musicians, and humankind in general. Few things are more beautiful than the evening song of the wood thrush as it echoes from deep within the forest. These birds are capable of producing an especially amazing sound thanks to the way their vocal organs are designed—a single wood thrush can actually sing two different notes at the same time, creating beautiful harmony. Once you hear the song, patiently scan the upper and inner branches of the forest for this rusty brown master singer. Wood thrushes have suffered severe declines in population during the past thirty years due to loss of habitat, forest fragmentation, and nest parasitism from the brown-headed cowbird, which will actually lay its own eggs in the wood thrush nest.

HOW DO I IDENTIFY IT? This medium-sized brown thrush (7¾ inches long) has a bright rufous head and neck, an olive brown back and tail, and a white breast with large dark spots. Erect and robinlike in its posture, the wood thrush sings a multi-pitched and highly variable *eeeolay* song and utters a *whit-whit-whit* call when it's agitated. Wood thrush males do most of their singing at dawn and dusk, usually from a mid-level perch in the forest.

WHERE DO I FIND IT? From spring through fall your best chance of spotting a wood thrush is to listen for a male singing from patches of dense forest. Wood thrushes spend only their summers with us in eastern North America, arriving as early as April, but departing for the tropics by mid-August or later. Many make the flight across the Gulf of Mexico in both spring and fall. During the breeding season, they can be found in mixed deciduous forests with tall trees and a thick understory. Fragmented forest plots or those with cleared understory (due to deer browsing or human landscaping) are far less attractive to wood thrushes.

WHAT CAN I FEED OR DO TO ATTRACT IT? Feeding much like a robin on the forest floor, the wood thrush sweeps aside leaf litter with its bill to uncover insects, larvae, millipedes, moths, ants, and even salamanders and snails. In fall, wood thrushes will feed in forest-edge habitats to take advantage of fruits and berries. Consider adding raspberry, blackberry, and gooseberry plants to your backyard garden to help attract wood thrushes. Fruit-bearing dogwoods are also a big hit with these birds. Wood thrushes are not likely to visit a feeder, but you may see them running along your lawn like a robin. Wood thrushes can be attracted to backyard water features for feeding and bathing. If you live near a woodland patch, you will very likely hear wood thrushes singing from your backyard.

NESTING The female wood thrush builds a cup-shaped nest out of grasses, leaves, and rootlets, usually held together with mud, in the fork of a tree branch within 20 feet of the ground. She lays three to four eggs and incubates them for about 12 days before they hatch. Young wood thrushes are ready to fledge two weeks later. Wood thrush nests in fragmented forest habitats are more likely to be parasitized by the brown-headed cowbird, which does not build its own nest, but rather lays its eggs in the nests of other songbirds—often at the expense of the host species.

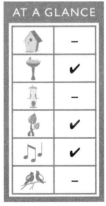

AT A GLANCE	
🏠	–
⛲	✔
🍽	–
🌿	✔
♫	✔
🐦🐦	–

American Robin

You don't need to be a bird watcher to know the American robin. Who hasn't seen one of these birds running along a lawn, pausing every so often to stare down an unlucky earthworm? The robin's familiar cheerily-cheerio *song meshes well with the thunk of basketballs and the drone of lawnmowers in suburban neighborhoods all across North America. You may be surprised to learn that American robins aren't robins at all—they are actually thrushes. What happened is this: When English settlers first visited the New World, they saw these red-breasted birds everywhere and were reminded of the similarly colored European robins from back home. So they started calling these new birds "robins" too. The name stuck. Many people consider robins to be a sign of spring, but the truth is that many robins stay in their home range*

year-round. They just tend to go unnoticed since they spend most of the winter months in woodlands looking for berries. As soon as the weather starts warming up again, the local robins reappear on lawns everywhere.

HOW DO I IDENTIFY IT?   These are fairly large, chunky songbirds that are dark grayish overall with red-orange underneath. Adult males sport brick-red breasts and black heads with a streaked white throat and lower belly. Females are paler overall. Young robins have heavy spots on the breast for their first few months out of the nest. Robins are very vocal birds, often the first to sing in the wee hours of the morning and the last to quiet down at night. Listen for their *puk-puk-puk* calls year-round.

WHERE DO I FIND IT?   You don't need to look far. The robin is basically a bird of lawns with trees and shrubs, though it also breeds in high mountain forests near clear-cuts or openings. Few other species show its adaptability to diverse habitats, from landscaped parking lot islets to dense, secluded forests. In winter, look for these birds in woodlands where berries are plentiful.

WHAT CAN I FEED OR DO TO ATTRACT IT?   By mowing the lawn regularly and planting dense evergreens and fruit-bearing shrubs and trees, we unintentionally provide perfect conditions for robins. This is one reason why these birds are so plentiful throughout much of their range. They seldom visit feeders but will eat bread, chopped raisins, grapes, and crumbled, moistened dog chow in severe winter weather. Robins gather in large flocks in fall and winter to raid fruiting trees and shrubs, fluttering and giggling as they reach for food. They are especially attracted to crabapples, Virginia creeper, honeysuckle, and wild strawberry plants.

NESTING   You may be familiar with the robin's sturdy mud-and-grass cup, often nestled in an evergreen, a climbing vine, on a horizontal branch, or even on a windowsill or porch light. The female incubates three to four bluish eggs for about two weeks. Adults can be seen running around with bills full of earthworms as soon as the young hatch. The young leave the nest, barely able to flutter, on about the thirteenth day. You can recognize them by their spotted, whitish breasts and reedy, begging calls. The male feeds them for another three weeks, while the female usually starts a second family. By planting junipers and spruces, you can provide year-round shelter for robins and also increase the chances of them nesting in your yard.

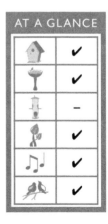

AT A GLANCE	
🏠	✔
🛁	✔
🔦	–
🌿	✔
♫	✔
🐦	✔

Gray Catbird

Named for its mewing, catlike call, the catbird is actually a multi-talented singer that is almost comparable to the mockingbird in its vocal versatility. The male catbird makes an almost endless array of sounds, one after the other; some are his own and others are "stolen" from other birds or even from frogs, domestic animals, or mechanical devices heard in his travels. Not a bad resume for an otherwise plain gray bird. The female catbird will even chime in from time to time. In most of its U.S. range, the catbird is migratory, moving southward in winter, away from the coldest weather. Flying at night, migrant catbirds are often victims of collision, striking tall buildings or communication towers with distressing frequency. A few avoid the dangers of migration by remaining in their northern territories, a tactic that works if they are well fed and the season is not overly harsh.

HOW DO I IDENTIFY IT? A slim, slate-gray bird about 9 inches long, the catbird is distinguished by a solid black cap and a bright chestnut patch under its tail. Because of its habit of cocking its tail, this patch is often visible. Catbirds are easy to recognize because—no matter what age, sex, or season—they all look the same. Like other mimics (birds that copy the sounds they hear), these birds are very talkative. You can usually tell a catbird's song from that of other mimics, though, because each phrase is repeated only once, and its telltale *meouw* is thrown in from time to time.

WHERE DO I FIND IT? Gray catbirds spend the summer throughout most of the eastern two-thirds of the United States, avoiding the southernmost states until winter. They can be found year-round along the Atlantic coast. Although gray catbirds are common, they can be easy to miss because of their secretive nature. Look for them in brushy areas, along woodland edges, and in suburban areas where there are lots of shrubs. Despite their energetic, talkative nature, catbirds tend to be loners. You don't usually see a flock of catbirds except when the birds are migrating, and even then, they tend to limit their group to about ten birds.

WHAT CAN I FEED OR DO TO ATTRACT IT? Foraging in thickets and brambles, the gray catbird eats mostly insects in spring and summer, adding small fruits as fall approaches. Favored insects include caterpillars, ants, aphids, termites, cicadas, and dragonflies. Among fruits, it chooses grapes, cherries, and berries, followed by such late-lingering items as multiflora rosehips, catbrier, privet berries, bittersweet, and mountain ash. If a catbird remains in your neighborhood during winter, it may be attracted by offerings of dried or fresh fruit, suet, doughnuts, peanut hearts, or table scraps. These birds are easily intimidated by other species, so they are more likely to respond to food scattered on the ground than concentrated in a small feeding dish.

NESTING Singing from deep within a thicket, the male catbird courts his female in spring. After mating, she builds a bulky cup of twigs, weeds, and leaves, sometimes adding bits of paper or string and then lining it with fine grasses or hair. She incubates her three or four eggs for about two weeks; both parents then feed the nestlings for 10 to 12 days until they fledge. Two broods are common.

Northern Mockingbird

This formerly southern species has been expanding its range for a century and now covers nearly every corner of the United States. Its rich, warbling voice and uncanny ability to imitate the calls of other birds—not to mention rusty hinges, frogs, dogs, and squeaky wheels—make it a superstar in any avian chorus. Even the most experienced bird watcher will confess to being occasionally fooled by a mocker's convincing rendition of a wood-pewee's song or a scarlet tanager's call. A single mockingbird may learn up to two hundred different songs during its lifetime. The mockingbird's spectacular talent has not gone unnoticed; five different states have chosen this popular songster as their state bird!

HOW DO I IDENTIFY IT? The mockingbird is fairly large (9 to 11 inches long) with medium gray upperparts and a pale breast and belly. Its long tail is edged in white, and there are prominent white patches on the wings that are especially visible in flight. The bill and legs are black. The sexes are alike. This bird's voice more than makes up for its lack of colorful plumage. It is loud, clear, and—in spring and summer—nearly incessant. When the moon is bright, mockingbirds will sing at night. The mockingbird tends to repeat each phrase three times before moving on to the next. Both males and females sing.

WHERE DO I FIND IT? These birds can be found throughout most of the United States. Mockers like to feed in short-grass areas with shrubby edges, so look for them in suburban towns, open city parks, small family farms, hedgerows, backyards, and similar locations. They are nonmigratory, present year-round in the areas they inhabit.

WHAT CAN I FEED OR DO TO ATTRACT IT? The diet of the mockingbird is composed of insects (spring and summer) and fruits (summer, fall, and winter). Earthworms, spiders, snails, and other small, meaty prey round out the menu. Multiflora rosehips are a mainstay in winter, and the range expansion of the mockingbird may have coincided with the spread of this alien plant. Though mockingbirds do not eat the usual feeder fare, they may be attracted, especially in winter, with offerings of suet, peanut butter, doughnuts, or small fruits. This is not always a good idea, however, for mockers are very territorial, and individual birds may defend a winter feeding area against all other species. If this happens, the easiest solution is to hang feeders on all sides of your house, so the aggressive mockingbird cannot see and defend all of them at once.

NESTING During spring courtship, a male mockingbird sings almost around the clock, often from a high perch, all the while jumping up in the air and waving his wings. When a female responds, both partners build the nest, a bulky mass of twigs around a cup of softer plant material, lined with moss and animal hair. Three to four eggs are laid and incubated by the female for about two weeks. The nestlings are fed by both parents for 12 days until fledging, and for about two weeks after as they learn to fend for themselves. You can provide good cover and nesting sites for mockingbirds by planting perennial vines, such as grapes, wintercreepers, Virginia creepers, and honeysuckles. The birds may also eat the fruits of these plants, so it's a win-win situation.

European Starling

In 1889, there were no European starlings in North America, yet today—just over a century later—we have more than two hundred million. Blame a fan of William Shakespeare. In 1890, a flock of a hundred starlings was released in New York's Central Park in an attempt to bring to America all the bird species mentioned in Shakespeare's plays. The adaptable starling soon spread westward in one of history's greatest avian population explosions. You are not likely to ever encounter a quiet starling—these birds are incredibly vocal, displaying an astonishing ability to mimic other bird songs, sirens, voices, barks, or mechanical sounds. They do this year-round and can be very convincing at times. In fact, if you think you may be hearing the song of a meadowlark or some other bird during the dead of winter when most songbirds are not singing, look around for a talented starling instead.

HOW DO I IDENTIFY IT?   These medium-sized birds (8½ inches long) are glossy black overall with a bright yellow bill during spring and summer. Up close, you can see the green and purple in the starling's iridescent plumage. In winter, starlings are duller overall, covered with white spots (little stars, or "starlings") with a blackish bill. Starlings are almost always found in flocks. In flight, they flap their triangular-shaped wings rapidly.

WHERE DO I FIND IT?   Most Americans can see a starling simply by looking out their window. These birds cover the entire North American continent year-round, except for the far North in winter. Starlings can be found in just about every habitat type, though they are most common in areas where humans are present, such as farms, cities, and suburbs. They are least common in remote, pristine habitats. In fall, starlings form gigantic, noisy flocks roaming in search of food and roosting sites. These flocks can be made up of hundreds of thousands of birds.

WHAT CAN I FEED OR DO TO ATTRACT IT?   Many bird watchers consider starlings a pest at their feeders and birdhouses. To discourage starlings at your feeder, simply remove the foods they prefer: suet, peanuts, bread, and cracked corn. (If, instead, you'd like to attract more starlings to your backyard, simply do the opposite!) When not visiting feeders, starlings keep a regular diet of insects, berries, fruits, and seeds, but they are not picky eaters—they're just as willing to eat French fries from a dumpster as they are to find bugs on our lawns or suet at our feeders. The starling's traditional foraging technique is to insert its long, sharp bill into the ground and then open it to expose beetle grubs and other prey.

NESTING   Starlings are cavity nesters that cannot excavate their own holes, so they use existing cavities, such as woodpecker holes, pipes, crevices in buildings, and birdhouses. Sites are often stolen from other, less aggressive cavity nesters, such as bluebirds or purple martins. (To exclude starlings from your nest boxes, make sure the entry holes are 1⁹⁄₁₆ inches or less in diameter.) Once a male has a site, a female will help finish the nest—a messy affair of grass, feathers, paper, and plastic. Between four to six eggs are laid and incubated by both parents for about 12 days. Young starlings leave the nest three weeks later.

Cedar Waxwing

A beady, insect-like trill first alerts many bird watchers to the presence of cedar waxwings, as they tend to completely blend into the surrounding foliage. These wandering fruit-eaters appear and disappear seemingly without rhyme or reason, descending to strip a tree of its fruits and then whirling off to parts unknown. Fermented fruits sometimes cause entire flocks of waxwings to stagger about on the ground until their intoxication wears off. Cedar waxwings travel in tight flocks to locate and feed on small fruits. They may be completely hidden in leaves as they flutter and pluck fruit, only to explode out with reedy calls and a rush of wings when startled. In late summer, they may be seen in twisting, dodging pursuits of winged insects over water. Waxwings get their name from the red secretions on the tips of their wing feathers, which look like shiny drops of sealing wax. Worldwide, there are only two other species of waxwing: the Bohemian and Japanese waxwings. Waxwings are related to silky flycatchers, a largely tropical family of birds.

HOW DO I IDENTIFY IT?   Overall, these birds are medium-sized (about 7 inches long), dressed in a warm, brownish gray plumage, and have crests like cardinals and blue jays. "Sleek" is the word most often used to describe the silky fawn plumage of the cedar waxwing. A velvety black bandit mask hides the eyes, and a bright yellow band tips the gray tail. You may occasionally encounter a cedar waxwing with orange rather than yellow tail tips. This is caused by the bird's diet. When a young, developing waxwing eats the red fruit of certain honeysuckle species, it grows orange tail feathers.

WHERE DO I FIND IT?   The cedar waxwing's only real habitat requirement is the presence of fruit-bearing trees and shrubs, so it can be found everywhere except grasslands, deserts, and deep interior forests. Thought to be nomadic, the species does make a poorly understood migration that takes it as far south as southern Central America. Cedar waxwings are most often seen in flocks in fall and winter.

WHAT CAN I FEED OR DO TO ATTRACT IT?   These birds are not likely to visit your bird feeders. Attracting cedar waxwings is best accomplished by planting the trees and shrubs they prefer—serviceberry, hawthorn, firethorn, dogwood, chokecherry, viburnum, native honeysuckle, blueberry, cedar, and others that bear small fruits. They may also visit birdbaths, especially those with moving water.

NESTING   While many bird species are strongly territorial, cedar waxwings do not defend a territory at all. In fact, they are sometimes semi-colonial, nesting close together with other waxwing neighbors. However, these birds are monogamous. Both sexes help build a bulky, cup-shaped nest in the outer canopy of a tree. Leaves, straw, twigs, and string are used to construct the nest. Sometimes waxwings gather these materials by stealing from other birds' nests. The female lays four eggs and incubates them for 12 days, while the male feeds her. Young are fed on insects for the first two days, then solely on regurgitated fruits, leaving the nest around 15 days later. This fruit-based diet ensures that any parasitic brown-headed cowbirds hatching in their nests do not survive. Large flocks of immature birds (identifiable by their yellowish, streaked bellies) linger near breeding grounds for one or two months after the adults leave.

AT A GLANCE

	–
	✔
	–
	✔
	✔
	–

Yellow-rumped Warbler

Warblers are some of the coolest birds around. Ask a bird watcher what it was that got them hooked on birding, and many of them will probably mention going on a bird walk in April and May during the peak of spring migration and being overwhelmed by the sheer beauty and diversity of this interesting group of birds. Most warblers are colorful, great singers, and highly migratory. Because of their migratory nature and because they are mostly insect-eaters, warblers are not often thought of as backyard birds. Most people hit the local park or find a good nature trail to see warblers. However, many of these birds do pass through North American backyards during spring and fall, often completely unnoticed. One of the most widespread and numerous of these warblers—and the most likely one to encounter in your backyard—is the yel-low-rumped warbler, a.k.a. "butterbutt." Yellow-rumped warblers found in western states look a little different from their eastern counterparts—in fact, they used to be considered two separate species.

HOW DO I IDENTIFY IT? Butterbutts are 5 to 6 inches long, with a sharp thin bill and slightly notched tail. In spring and summer, the male is blue-gray with either a white (eastern birds) or yellow (western birds) throat and white belly, black streaking on its back, a black face patch, two white wing bars, black bib, and yellow spots on the crown, shoulders, and rump. Spring females are browner and duller than their mates. Immatures and fall adults are brown above, with brown-streaked underparts and little or no yellow visible. Despite that long list of markings and plumage variations, there's really just one thing you need to look for: the bright yellow rump. That, along with a frequent and distinctive *check!* note, will quickly identify these birds year-round.

WHERE DO I FIND IT? These birds breed in the far North and throughout much of the western United States. In the East, they are known only as a migrant or winter resident. Migrants can be found in backyards, woodlands, hedgerows, thickets, and even along beaches as they stream through in large flocks. Winter birds congregate wherever they can find berries, their primary cold-weather food. Yellow-rumped warblers can be found year-round in parts of the West.

WHAT CAN I FEED OR DO TO ATTRACT IT? Though not common feeder birds, yellow-rumped warblers will sometimes visit bird feeders for sunflower seed bits, suet or suet dough, raisins, and fruit. They've also been known to raid hummingbird feeders for sugar water. The best way to attract these birds is by providing natural food via fruit-producing plants—bayberries and junipers are their favorites. Yellow-rumps also readily visit backyard water features for drinking and bathing.

NESTING For nesting, the yellow-rumped warbler selects conifer forests, generally spruce, pine, or cedar. The female builds the nest on a horizontal branch, anywhere from 5 to 50 feet high in the tree, using bark, twigs, weeds, and roots to create an open cup that is then lined with hair and feathers. The female incubates the four or five eggs for 12 to 13 days. When the chicks hatch, both parents feed them for 10 to 12 days until fledging, and then the male feeds them for a time afterward. There are usually two broods per year.

AT A GLANCE

🏠	–
🛁	✔
🗼	✔
🌹	✔
🎵	✔
🐦	✔

Scarlet Tanager

If you think you may have seen a cardinal with black wings, chances are you saw a scarlet tanager. With a solid scarlet-red body and jet-black wings and tail, the male scarlet tanager in its spring and summer plumage ranks among the most stunningly beautiful birds in North America. One glance at his neon-bright colors can turn even the most disinterested person into a passionate fan. These birds are also impressive long-distance migrants, flying thousands of miles each year between their summer range in eastern North America and their wintering grounds in the South American tropics. Oddly, this dazzling bird's song has been compared to "a robin with a sore throat." And although female birds do not usually sing, female scarlet tanagers actually do "sing" a short, soft version of their mates' songs.

HOW DO I IDENTIFY IT?   At just 7 inches long, scarlet tanagers are the smallest of our four North American tanager species. During spring and summer, the male scarlet tanager has a solid red body with jet-black wings and tail, black-button eyes, and a bone-gray bill. During fall and winter, he is a dull olive color with dark wings and pale yellow underparts. The female has the muted olive-yellow plumage year-round, and immature males resemble the females. In all plumages, the scarlet tanager's wings are darker than those of the summer tanager, our other eastern tanager species. (Male summer tanagers are completely red, with no black on the wings or tail.)

WHERE DO I FIND IT?   Look for scarlet tanagers in oak-dominated woodlands throughout eastern North America, mostly in southeastern Canada and the northeastern chunk of the United States. They arrive in April or May and depart by mid-autumn. A distinctive *chick-burr* call is often your first clue that a scarlet tanager is around. These birds can be easy to overlook in your backyard or along the hiking trail because they spend most of their time in the treetops, searching for insects and spiders. The females and immature males can be especially challenging to pick out because of their muted plumages, but, again, just listen for that distinctive *chick-burr* call and keep your eyes on the treetops.

WHAT CAN I FEED OR DO TO ATTRACT IT?   Because scarlet tanagers are mostly insect-eaters, they are a bit hard to please at the backyard feeder, although some will go for bread, doughnuts, orange halves, or a peanut butter–cornmeal mixture. You can also try offering them mealworms, which you can buy from your local seed supplier or bait shop. Berry-producing plants tend to lure scarlet tanagers down from the treetops—blueberries, mulberries, poison ivy berries, and multiflora rose are a few of their favorites—so try planting some of these in your backyard (well, maybe not poison ivy). Tanagers are also attracted to backyard water features, so keep a birdbath filled with water for them.

NESTING   If you live near a woodland patch, you may have tanagers nesting in or near your backyard. Scarlet tanagers typically nest high in a large deciduous tree—often, but not always, an oak. The female constructs a shallow nest of twigs, rootlets, weeds, and other plant material. Three to five eggs are laid, and the female incubates them for about two weeks. Both parents feed the nestlings for about 10 days and for two weeks more after the young leave the nest.

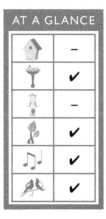

AT A GLANCE	
🏠	–
⛲	✔
🏮	–
🌿	✔
♪♩	✔
🐦🐦	✔

Spotted Towhee

If you look in a bird book published before 1995, you won't find the spotted towhee. Prior to that, the spotted towhee, a widespread and common bird of the West, was considered to be a western type of the rufous-sided towhee. After that we had two towhees with rufous sides: the spotted towhee (named for the large white spots on its black wings) and the eastern towhee. The name "towhee" comes from the call that these species make, which sounds like tow-hee! *or* chee-wink! *Towhees are actually large, ground-loving sparrows. They are nearly always found on or near the ground when foraging and even frequently nest on the ground. The exception may be during the spring courtship, when males sometimes sing from an exposed, elevated perch when trying to attract a mate.*

HOW DO I IDENTIFY IT?   A black hood around a bright red eye, bright white spots on a black back and wings, rufous sides, a pale belly, and a long black tail edged in white describes the male spotted towhee. Females are chocolate-brown on the head, back, wings, and tail where the males are black. Towhees have a large, dark bill. They are large birds (8 inches), looking much bigger and longer-tailed than most of their relatives in the sparrow family. The song of the spotted towhee is *chup-chup-chup-zreeee!* and its regular call is a rising, mewing *zreeee!*

WHERE DO I FIND IT?   Spotted towhees love a messy, brushy habitat. From the Central Great Plains west to southern British Columbia and south to Mexico, the spotted towhee is a common bird in chaparral, mesquite thickets, scrub habitats, and open woods with some brushy tangles. In particularly dense habitat, you might hear them calling or scratching on the ground before you spot them. They use their large feet to scratch aside leaf litter and ground cover, hoping to expose beetles, caterpillars, spiders, ants, and other goodies. Spotted towhees in arid portions of the West and along the Pacific coast are year-round residents. Birds that nest in the western Great Plains move south in winter. They are also common in winter on the southern Great Plains.

WHAT CAN I FEED OR DO TO ATTRACT IT?   If your property has an area of messy undergrowth or shrubby thickets, you've got prime spotted towhee habitat. If you do not have such habitat naturally, you can always use fallen or trimmed tree branches to create a brush pile, which towhees and many other birds will happily use. Towhees can be shy about coming very far out into the open. Since they love to scratch through leaf litter to find food, it's a good idea to let leaves and other natural ground cover accumulate. Mixed seed, cracked corn, millet, milo, and sunflower seeds scattered on the ground (or on a low platform feeder), especially near thick cover, will attract spotted towhees. Birdbaths with moving water are highly appealing to spotted towhees, too.

NESTING   Spotted towhees nest on or near the ground in a well-concealed spot, where the female builds a nest woven out of grass, rootlets, small twigs, and dried leaves. She lays three to six eggs and incubates them for about 12 days. Young towhees remain in the nest for about 10 days after hatching, during which time both parents share the feeding chores.

AT A GLANCE	
🏠	–
🏺	✔
🕯	✔
🌱	✔
♫	✔
🐦	✔

Eastern Towhee

Drink your TEA! *sings the eastern towhee throughout the brushy woodlands of the eastern United States. Formerly called the rufous-sided towhee (a much more descriptive name), this large sparrow (8½ inches long) is boldly patterned and spends nearly all its time on the ground scratching among the leaf litter, looking for food. The name towhee comes from the bird's call, which has also been transcribed as* chewink. *Many people know this bird as the chewink instead of towhee. Towhees' preference for thick cover and brushy habitat make them harder to see than other common species. The loud scratching of a foraging towhee sounds like a large animal walking through dry leaves; this is often your first clue to a towhee's presence. Some folks are reminded of a robin the first time they see a towhee because of the black and reddish orange color scheme, but towhees are smaller and more sparrow-shaped with a conspicuous white belly.*

HOW DO I IDENTIFY IT? Males are black above and white below with reddish orange sides. In flight, the birds' white wing and tail spots are noticeable. Female eastern towhees replace the male's black plumage areas with chocolate brown. In summer, recently fledged towhees can be confusing and hard to identify with their streaky, gray-brown coloring, but their white tail spots and ground-scratching habits will give them away. The spotted towhee in the West is very similar to the eastern towhee in habits and appearance, but spotted towhees have (wait for it) conspicuous white spots across the back and wings. The two species overlap only in a few parts of the central United States so confusing them is rarely an issue.

WHERE DO I FIND IT? Widespread across the eastern half of the United States and southern Canada, towhees in the northern part of the range are migratory, but those in the southern half are resident. Spring is the best time to find these birds. Male towhees are especially vocal during the breeding season and will leave deep cover to sing from a high perch within their territory. During mild winters, towhees may linger until harsh weather forces them to migrate or to seek the cover of wooded valleys and hollows. Brushy woodland thickets and edge habitats are preferred, but towhees are also found in older woodlands and suburban backyards.

WHAT CAN I FEED OR DO TO ATTRACT IT? Towhees eat just about anything found on the woodland floor, including insects, seeds, fruits, and even snails, spiders, and millipedes. They prefer to scratch the ground under feeding stations for mixed seeds, cracked corn, and sunflower seeds (which they crack open with their powerful bill). Offer seed on a platform feeder or directly on the ground to increase your chances of luring some towhees into your yard. Better yet, add a brush pile nearby to help these shy birds feel more at home.

AT A GLANCE	
🏠	–
🍶	✔
🪴	✔
🌳	✔
🎵	✔
🐦	✔

NESTING Towhees nest on or near the ground in a well-concealed spot. The female weaves a cup-shaped nest out of rootlets, bark strips, and grass. She also handles all the incubation duty, which typically lasts about 12 days. Normal clutch size is three to four eggs; young towhees fledge in about 10 days. Both towhee parents feed the youngsters, which allow the females to start a second—and sometimes a third—brood.

Chipping Sparrow

A close look at these natty little birds reveals much to admire in its quiet and confiding ways. As common as they are around backyards and parks, we know surprisingly little about the chipping sparrow's mating habits. One Ontario study showed males not to be monogamous, as assumed, but to mate freely. These birds have the interesting habit of lining their nests with animal hair. They'll also use human hair, but more on that later.

HOW DO I IDENTIFY IT?   A rusty beret and bold, white eyeline are the best field marks of this slender little sparrow. Plain gray underparts, a streaked brown back, and a small, all-black bill set off its striking head markings. The chipping sparrow is one of our smallest sparrows (about 5½ inches long). It is an underappreciated bird, perhaps because it is so small and unobtrusive. Listen for its rather dry, monotonous trills (sometimes compared to the sound of a sewing machine) as well as its signature chipping notes.

WHERE DO I FIND IT?   In summer, these birds are found throughout Canada and much of the United States. They can be found year-round in the southeastern United States. Before the massive expansion of suburbs, chipping sparrows were limited to open, grassy coniferous forests and parklike woodlands with shrubby understories. Our suburban habitats have just the right mix of short grass, shrubbery, and conifers that chipping sparrows need, so we can enjoy their company on our doorsteps and sidewalks. Although northern populations are strongly migratory, southern birds flock up but tend to stay near their breeding grounds. Winter flocks of up to fifty birds perch in trees, descending en masse to the ground to peck for seeds and then adjourning to treetops before the next feeding bout.

WHAT CAN I FEED OR DO TO ATTRACT IT?   Chipping sparrows forage primarily on or near the ground, feasting on weed and grass seeds and some smaller fruits. They're easy to please at backyard feeding stations, with black-oil sunflower seeds and cracked corn being among their favorite feeder foods. Chipping sparrows also love mixed seeds, suet, rolled oats, and mealworms. They'll come to hopper-style feeders or feed directly on the ground. Bird feeders aren't the only way to cater to backyard chipping sparrows. These birds also greatly appreciate baked and crushed eggshells strewn on a sidewalk. But it's most fun to offer them human or pet hair clippings. A trip to any salon can net a season's worth, and you may have the pleasure of finding a used nest lined with your own hair—the ultimate vanity piece for the discerning homeowner.

NESTING   Planting shrubs and vines—such as creepers and honeysuckles—can increase the chances of these birds nesting in your yard. Female chipping sparrows weave lovely little nests of thin twigs and weed stems, with a center composed of animal hair. These are often concealed in low trees and shrubs, but are easily located by the shrilling of older nestlings. Females incubate the four eggs for around 12 days, and the young leave the nest about 9 to 12 days later. Chipping sparrows feed insects to their young, sometimes flycatching on the wing. Streaky, brown, and nondescript, the young are fed by their parents for three more weeks before forming juvenile flocks.

AT A GLANCE	
🏠	–
💧	✔
🌿	✔
🧍	✔
🎵	✔
🐦	–

American Tree Sparrow

You're most likely to encounter American tree sparrows during the winter months, when they abandon their summer home in the Arctic and migrate into southern Canada and the northern two-thirds of the United States. In winter, these birds become quite common in open fields, brushy areas, and just about any backyard with a well-stocked feeding station. The "tree" part of this bird's name is misleading—woodlands and forests are some of the last places you're likely to find an American tree sparrow. In fact, these birds nest in the northernmost areas of the Arctic tundra, where there are few trees at all. They were named by early European settlers who were reminded of the Eurasian tree sparrow of the Old World (there is a superficial resemblance between the two species). As the saying goes, the rest was history.

HOW DO I IDENTIFY IT?   The American tree sparrow is a small gray bird (5½ inches long) with a bright rufous crown and an obvious black splotch on the center of an otherwise unmarked breast. The bird's cone-shaped bill is conspicuously two-toned, with dark above and yellow below. The back and wings are handsomely marked with rust, gray, and white. Because songbirds generally sing only on their breeding grounds, and American tree sparrows breed in the Arctic, you're not likely to hear the male's sweet, whistling song in your backyard. But you may hear the soft call notes given between tree sparrows in a foraging winter flock.

WHERE DO I FIND IT?   Don't look for these birds in areas with lots of trees. You're much better off looking in old, brushy fields with a good supply of weeds (these birds feed heavily on weed seeds). American tree sparrows are found in flocks ranging from only a dozen to more than two hundred birds. Look along the ground near brushy areas and listen for the birds' soft call notes. When flushed from the ground, they tend to fly up and perch in a nearby tree, where they are easy to spot. Perhaps the best place to look for American tree sparrows is at a bird feeder—in many areas, these are very common winter feeder birds.

WHAT CAN I FEED OR DO TO ATTRACT IT?   From late fall to early spring, American tree sparrows flock to backyard bird feeders throughout southern Canada and much of the United States. They are most attracted to white proso millet, which is found in most good seed mixes. They may also eat sunflower chips, cracked corn, and suet. American tree sparrows are ground feeders, so offer seed either directly on the ground or on a platform feeder. Away from the feeding station, these birds feed heavily on weed seeds, so a yard with dandelions, goldenrods, coneflowers, and various grasses is likely to attract decent numbers of tree sparrows.

NESTING   Back home in the northernmost regions of the continent, American tree sparrows construct nests of grasses, twigs, and moss on or near the ground. Females incubate three to five brownish eggs for about 12 days, and the young leave the nest when they're about 8 days old. After a few more days, the young tree sparrows are able to fly but are still fed by the parents for about two more weeks before gaining full independence.

Field Sparrow

The field sparrow's clear, whistled notes of a single tone is an easy bird song to learn and remember. Listen throughout the day, even in summer, for this persistent singer. Its rhythmic pattern sounds like a ping-pong ball being dropped onto a table. A subtly beautiful sparrow of farm pastures and shrubby old meadows, the field sparrow is common in rural areas of the eastern two-thirds of the United States. Within its breeding range, any older farm field should host field sparrows. During the 1800s, the field sparrow population flourished as forests were cleared for farming, creating ideal conditions for them. Today, though field sparrows are still common, they appear to be on the decline, probably because most old, brushy fields are either growing back into forest or are being cleared for agriculture or suburban development.

HOW DO I IDENTIFY IT?   The field sparrow is a small bird (5¾ inches long) with a biggish bill and long tail, but the first field marks most bird watchers notice are the pink bill, plain face, and white ring surrounding the dark eye. Telling the field sparrow apart from chipping or tree sparrows is a matter of noting the field's unmarked buffy-gray breast and indistinct head stripes of brown and gray.

WHERE DO I FIND IT?   As its name suggests, the field sparrow is found in fields, but it prefers brushy, older fields that have the beginnings of reforestation—saplings, small shrubs, and large thick clumps of grass. Field sparrows are found all across the eastern United States, but—unlike many of our migrant songbirds—they may only migrate a few hundred miles to spend the winter. In spring and summer, males do their singing from an exposed perch within their territories. Look for them perched on top of saplings or fence posts.

WHAT CAN I FEED OR DO TO ATTRACT IT?   Field sparrows will come to cracked corn, mixed seeds, and eggshell bits scattered on the ground beneath bird feeders. Throughout the year, the field sparrow's diet is grass seeds and other small plant seeds; in spring and summer the diet shifts to insects. Moths, grasshoppers, flies, and other grassland insects make up half of their summer diet, with most of the insects being found on or near the ground. Letting a portion of your yard or lawn grow up into a weedy patch is a good way to attract field sparrows. In winter, as flocks of field sparrows forage together, a single bird will perch on top of a tall grass stem, letting its weight bend the stalk to the ground where the seeds can more easily be eaten.

NESTING   In early spring field sparrow nests are built on the ground, near a grass clump or small shrub. Later nests may be in taller shrubs or vegetation, but the construction is the same—a loosely woven outer cup of grass lined with fine, soft grasses, all built by the female. Three to six eggs are laid and incubated by the female for about 12 days. Like other ground nesters, young field sparrows develop quickly and may leave the nest within a week. The birds are able to fly after about two weeks, with the parents still tending to their needs. Fledgling field sparrows look quite different from their parents and can be hard to identify when seen alone. After another two weeks with their parents, the young birds attain full independence.

AT A GLANCE	
🐦	–
🛁	✔
🏠	✔
🌿	✔
🎵	✔
🐦🐦	–

Song Sparrow

These are among the most common birds in North America. Most brownish striped sparrows you see are going to be song sparrows. Look for them in a variety of habitats, from brushy fields to woodland edges to suburban back-yards. True to its name, song sparrows sing often, sometimes year-round. If there's a resident song sparrow in your yard, you'll probably hear is cheery notes at first light—as reliable as, but more pleasant than, a rooster's. One of the best-studied birds in North America, the song sparrow was the subject of Margaret Morse Nice's groundbreaking behavioral study in the 1930s. Much of what scientists understand about how songbirds choose and defend territories began with this study.

HOW DO I IDENTIFY IT?   The plumage of song sparrows varies widely throughout the continent, but always look for a smallish brown and gray streaky sparrow (6 inches long) with a long tail. Their white breasts are heavily streaked and marked with a messy central spot. A grayish, striped face and crown and warm-brown upperparts complete the description. Flight is low and jerky, with the tail twisting distinctively. Three introductory notes leading to a variable jumble of trills and chips distinguish its song. Males and females look similar.

WHERE DO I FIND IT?   Though song sparrows occupy a wide range of habitats, they are most often found in shrubbery near water, from small streams to beach habitats. Often you will find them walking along the water's edge like a sandpiper. Song sparrows tend to be migratory in northern areas and year-round residents in the southern United States; this varies by population. The song sparrow is one of the most variable songbirds known. Birds in the Pacific Northwest, for example, are larger, darker, and heavier-billed compared to Southeastern coastal song sparrows. There may be as many as thirty different types of song sparrows in North America.

WHAT CAN I FEED OR DO TO ATTRACT IT?   Song sparrows readily visit bird feeders for sunflower seeds, cracked corn, and mixed seeds. They'll spend a lot of time on the ground under your feeders, looking for dropped seeds. Peanut butter–based suet mixes are a favorite food, and song sparrows will appear to beg at windows for such tasty fare. The song sparrow's diet varies seasonally, with insects being its primary prey in spring and summer and with seeds and fruits dominating in fall and winter. Most of the song sparrow's foraging takes place on the ground, where it will scratch and kick about in leaf litter and grasses for weed seeds and insects.

NESTING   The persistent singing of song sparrows is linked to strong territorial behavior; where they are resident year-round, they tend to defend territories year-round. Territory boundaries are quite stable from year to year. Both sexes defend their territory, and they tend to stay with one mate. Females construct a bulky nest of bark strips and weed and grass stems, well hidden deep in a dense shrub. Small, ornamental evergreens are irresistible to song sparrows. The female incubates three to five eggs for about 13 days. Young birds leave the nest at only 10 days and may be fed by the parents for the next 20 days before they are fully independent. They are fond of water and will often nest near a water garden or backyard pond.

AT A GLANCE	
🏠	–
🍸	✔
🪹	✔
🌺	✔
🎵	✔
🐦	–

White-throated Sparrow

Old Sam Peabody, Peabody, Peabody *is the sweet whistled song of the white-throated sparrow. In Canada, where this species spends the breeding season, the song is transcribed as* Oh sweet Canada, Canada, Canada—*but there's no arguing that the white-throated sparrow's song is easy to recognize and one of the most interesting musical sounds of the avian world. From September to March these northern breeders occupy the eastern United States, in loose flocks with other sparrows, brightening winter days with their cheery sounds. Look for white-throated sparrows on the ground beneath your feeders from late fall through early spring. If your feeders are some distance from cover, consider moving them closer to the woods' edge or adding a brush pile nearby to make woodland birds (such as white-throated sparrows) feel more at home.*

HOW DO I IDENTIFY IT?   The first field mark most people notice on the white-throated sparrow is not the white throat but the black-and-white striped head pattern with a yellow spot between the eyes and bill. Even at a distance this striking pattern is obvious. Some white-throated sparrows have tan-striped heads and a tannish throat. These belong to the tan-striped variety of the species (though at one time, the common belief was that these were young birds not yet in adult plumage). This medium-sized sparrow (6¾ inches long) has a gray breast and a brown, lightly patterned back.

WHERE DO I FIND IT?   Spending most of the summer in the coniferous forests of the far north and New England, white-throated sparrows spend fall and winter far to the south, where they are regulars at bird feeders and in brushy edge habitats. They can be found in the New England states year-round. They prefer a habitat with thick underbrush and are found near the edge of the woods, along hedgerows, and in brushy thickets in parks and backyards. Listen for their loud, sharp *chink* calls as they move about in winter flocks, often hidden from view.

WHAT CAN I FEED OR DO TO ATTRACT IT?   White-throated sparrows prefer to feed on the ground. In spring and summer, the white-throated sparrow's diet is focused on insects and arachnids—ants, grubs, and spiders—that it uncovers as it scratches through the leaf litter, much like a towhee does. In fall, the diet shifts to include berries; in winter, it includes mostly seeds from grasses. At bird feeders white-throated sparrows are attracted to mixed seed, cracked corn, and sunflower or peanut bits. But their real favorite is white proso millet—that small, round, cream-colored seed found in most basic seed mixes. (You can also buy white millet by itself from many seed suppliers.) Try offering seed on a platform feeder or directly on the ground to make your feeding station especially accommodating for these birds.

NESTING   White-throated sparrows nest on or near the ground in a well-concealed spot. The cup-shaped nest is built by the female from grass, pine needles, and twigs and lined with soft material, such as rootlets or fur. The female incubates the four to five eggs for about two weeks; the male assists her in feeding the nestlings for the nine days prior to fledging. The young birds rely on the parents for food for about another two weeks.

AT A GLANCE	
🏠	–
🍸	✔
🧴	✔
🐦	✔
🎵	✔
🐦🐦	–

Dark-eyed Junco

Most Americans are familiar with the dark-eyed junco. Even those who don't watch birds often have probably noticed these common gray-and-white birds in their backyards. Dark-eyed juncos are often called "snowbirds" because they seem to show up at our feeders and in our backyards at the same time as the first snows begin falling over much of the country. For many of us, winter is the only time we have dark-eyed juncos around. They form large flocks in backyards, parks and pastures and along rural roadsides and woodland edges in just about every corner of the United States except southern Florida. Watch for the flash of white from their tail feathers as they dart between brush piles or scatter from feeding on the ground beneath a bird feeder.

HOW DO I IDENTIFY IT? Juncos are medium-sized sparrows (6¼ inches long), but unlike most sparrows, their plumage lacks streaking. Dark gray above and white below (or "gray skies above, snow below"), the junco has a cone-shaped, pinkish bill and flashes its white outer tail feathers in flight. Male juncos in the East are a darker gray than the overall brownish-colored females. Western juncos show a variety of plumage colors, and many of these color forms were considered separate species until recently. Now they are all lumped into a single species: dark-eyed junco. Juncos make a variety of sounds, all of them high-pitched tinkling trills, especially when flushed from cover. Their songs are very similar to those of the chipping sparrow—sometimes it's difficult to tell the two species apart when you can't see the singer.

WHERE DO I FIND IT? These birds can be found throughout most of North America at some point in the year. In winter, they can be found in every state. Look for them in brushy areas, fields, and, of course, your backyard. They are often seen scratching through leaf litter, grass, or snow when looking for food. In spring, most juncos retreat to the far-north woods of Canada to breed, though the New England states and some areas in the West have juncos year-round. Spring migration begins as early as March and continues through early June. Fall migration occurs from mid-August through October.

WHAT CAN I FEED OR DO TO ATTRACT IT? Juncos find their food on the ground, so in backyards they tend to hang around beneath bird feeders, picking through dropped seeds. They love white millet, which is found in most mixed wild birdseed blends and can also be purchased separately. Place some millet on a platform feeder or directly on the ground for best results. Another effective way to attract juncos is by building a brush pile near your feeding station. In spring and summer, juncos shift their diet from seeds to mostly insects, including caterpillars, grasshoppers, and spiders, and berries.

NESTING The junco's nest is a simple, open cup of grasses and leaves, loosely woven and lined with finer grasses, fur, or feathers. Nests are normally located on the ground in a concealed spot and built by the female. She incubates her three to five eggs for almost two weeks; the male helps with feeding chores once the young hatch. Within two weeks the young birds leave the nest, and the parents are free to start another brood if the season permits.

AT A GLANCE	
🏠	–
🏺	✔
🧂	✔
🌾	✔
♪	✔
🐦	✔

Northern Cardinal

Cardinals are the familiar and beloved "redbird" found all across the eastern United States. This bird is so popular that seven U.S. states and countless sports teams have chosen the cardinal as their official emblem. In spring and summer, cardinal pairs can be found together, often with the male perched high above, singing his what-cheer-cheer-cheer song. In fall and winter, cardinals can be found in large loose flocks, especially during harsh weather. Nothing brightens up a snowy winter scene quite like a flock of bright red male cardinals dotting the landscape. You can enjoy these birds all year long in your backyard by offering them the four things they need to survive: food, water, a place to roost, and a place to nest. A few bird feeders, a chemical-free

lawn and garden, and some thick brushy cover will suit their requirements nicely. Watch for cardinals early and late—they are often the first birds active at dawn and the last ones to "turn in" at dusk.

HOW DO I IDENTIFY IT? A black face and a long red crest smartly set off the bright red plumage of the male cardinal. Females are a muted, brownish version of the male. Strongly territorial, mated cardinal pairs will vigorously defend their nesting turf from rivals, even going so far as to attack their own reflections in windows, mistaking the image for another cardinal. One of the cardinal's most interesting behaviors is the "courtship kiss" in which a male feeds a bit of food to a female he is wooing. Male and female cardinals both sing.

WHERE DO I FIND IT? These birds are resident throughout the eastern United States. Found in a variety of habitats, from deserts to wetlands to manicured backyards, cardinals prefer an edge habitat—a place where woodland and open space meet. Listen for their loud, metallic chip calls. The cardinal's range has expanded northward in recent decades—thanks in part to the availability of food at bird feeders.

WHAT CAN I FEED OR DO TO ATTRACT IT? Cardinals absolutely love black-oil sunflower seed. Offer this in hopper-style feeders and on platform feeders and your backyard will be the most popular place in the neighborhood. Expand the menu with striped sunflower seed, safflower seed, suet, fruits, and peanuts. During the spring and summer, offer mealworms, which cardinals will readily accept as an additional protein source for their hungry young, to keep them coming to your yard. Cardinals tend to forage on or near the ground. Gardeners and homeowners appreciate cardinals for eating grubs, beetles, caterpillars, and other garden pests. In winter, cardinals shift to a greater reliance on seeds, nuts, and wild fruits. Backyards with fruit-bearing trees and shrubs like hollies, sumacs, cherries, and dogwoods tend to have the most cardinals year-round.

NESTING Female cardinals choose thick cover—vine or rose tangles or shrubs—in which to weave their shallow, cup-shaped nests out of grasses, rootlets, twigs, and bark strips. Into this nest, the female will lay three to five eggs and incubate them for nearly two weeks before they hatch. Both parents feed the youngsters for about 10 days before they fledge. In summer, young cardinals can often be seen following a parent around, begging to be fed. Males will take on this duty while the female starts a second brood.

AT A GLANCE

(birdhouse)	–
(birdbath)	✔
(feeder)	✔
(plant)	✔
(music notes)	✔
(birds)	✔

Rose-breasted Grosbeak

Rose-breasted grosbeaks are a welcome visitor to backyards across eastern North America. With its triangular scarlet breast patch and somewhat pen-guinlike pied plumage coloration, the male rose-breasted grosbeak is a North American beauty. This gorgeous songbird remains plentiful in a variety of habitats. The male's rich, musical song sounds like a more talented American robin. These birds have a distinctive chip *note that sounds a lot like a squeaky sneaker, once you learn this sound, you'll always know when there's a rose-breasted grosbeak around. Especially near the western edge of the breeding range, take a close look when identifying females and immature rose-breasted grosbeaks, which strongly resemble those of the closely related black-headed grosbeak, a western species. Fortunately for backyard bird watchers, there are only a few areas in the central United States where the two species are likely to be found together.*

HOW DO I IDENTIFY IT? Medium-sized (8 inches long), rose-breasted grosbeaks are songbirds with enormous finch-like bills. It is hard to mistake a male rose-breasted grosbeak. No other bird has a black head and back, a triangular rose-red breast patch, and a clear white belly. Equally striking in flight, the male flashes rose-red under his wings with a wide, rectangular white wing patch. The female has a dramatically different appearance. Looking like an overgrown brown-and-white finch, she is streaked below and has a broad white line above her eye and one below her dark ear patch. She can be easy to confuse with a female purple finch, but you can tell them apart by the grosbeak's larger size and white wing markings. In fall, immature males look similar but have an orangey wash across the underparts.

WHERE DO I FIND IT? They breed from far northwestern Canada throughout the Midwest and Northeast and at high elevations in the Appalachians. They prefer to nest in open, leafy woodlands or at the forest edge. You may find them in neighborhood parks, along wooded roadsides, and sometimes in suburban neighborhoods. On their wintering grounds in the tropics, rose-breasted grosbeaks tend to favor semi-open locales, sometimes with just scattered trees. During migration, they can show up just about anywhere, including your backyard. When not feasting on sunflower seeds at feeders or sampling the berries in your garden, these birds are most likely found up high, keeping a low profile near the treetops.

WHAT CAN I FEED OR DO TO ATTRACT IT? Rose-breasted grosbeaks come to feeders to dine on black-oil sunflower and safflower seeds. They will also eat shelled peanuts. With their versatile, heavy bills, these birds feed on both vegetable and animal matter. During spring and summer, rose-breasted grosbeaks eat a lot of insects, including beetles, bees, ants, bugs, and caterpillars. During fall migration, they mostly eat berries and seeds. Elderberry, Juneberry, raspberry, blackberry, and mulberry are some of the shrubs and small trees that can be planted to attract migrating rose-breasted grosbeaks.

NESTING A female grosbeak builds her nest in a tree or tall shrub, usually between 5 and 20 feet above the ground. Assisted a bit by the male, she works twigs, weeds, and leaves into the loosely woven open cup nest, then usually lays four eggs. Both parents incubate for about two weeks, then feed their nestlings, which leave the nest 9 to 12 days after hatching.

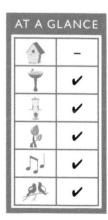

AT A GLANCE	
🏠	–
⛲	✔
⛲	✔
🌿	✔
🎵	✔
🐦	✔

Indigo Bunting

Appearing all black against the light, a male indigo bunting properly lit is an unforgettable sight. A persistent late-season singer, he sings a jingly song consisting of paired notes that are often described as Fire! Fire! Where? Where? Here! Here! Put it out! Put it out! *Much of what we know about celestial navigation in songbirds derives from work with captive indigo buntings at the Cornell Lab of Ornithology. Lucky is the one who hosts these brilliant birds in his or her backyard! Spring arrivals are most often first seen feasting on dandelion seeds. Later, black-oil sunflower seeds and millet mixes will keep these birds around. Indigo buntings are sometimes called the blue goldfinches; their shape, songs, and general habits are similar. If you're lucky enough to have a backyard full of both goldfinches and indigo buntings, you are living the dream.*

HOW DO I IDENTIFY IT?   The breathtaking, all-blue male indigo bunting, with his silvery conical bill, is unmistakable. Females and immatures are a warm cocoa-brown overall. This bunting has a habit of twitching its tail to the side, and its *spit!* note is distinctive. Males change their blue feathers for brown in autumn, which makes for some interestingly mottled individuals. They molt again on the wintering grounds and return in spring, blue once more.

WHERE DO I FIND IT?   This species is common by roadsides and disturbed areas where "trashy" vegetation flourishes. Power line cuts, old fields, landfills, railroads, and hedgerows ring with the songs of indigo buntings, especially as summer reaches its fullest. Look up high for the males singing from tall, exposed perches, and look down low for both males and females foraging close to the ground. Listen for those *spit!* calls. Indigo buntings are strongly migratory, wintering in central and northern South America.

WHAT CAN I FEED OR DO TO ATTRACT IT?   These birds really go for black-oil sunflower seed, sunflower hearts, and the millet from mixed seed. Like most other buntings and finches, indigos will also eat thistle seed (nyjer). Hopper-style and tube feeders tend to be the most attractive to buntings. The indigo bunting takes insects when they are available, especially to feed its nestlings. Weed seeds are its mainstay, supplemented by berries and small fruits. It forages on or near the ground, as well as in low shrubs and trees. Watch for them in autumn, bending grass stems and flicking their tails side to side as they forage in weedy patches. The growing popularity of "meadow in a can" seed mixtures make for rich feeding grounds for indigo buntings, which flock to coneflower, Mexican hat, cosmos, coreopsis, and especially foxtail grasses.

NESTING   Indigo buntings have a rather loose definition of monogamy, with extra-pair copulations being quite frequent. Males visit females in neighboring territories, and females visit males. Males vary in their tendency to feed young; some are attentive parents, whereas others leave most of the chick-rearing to their mates. The nest is bulky but compact, cup-shaped, and constructed of bark strips, grass and weed stems, and skeletonized leaves, all bound with spider webs. It's often low in blackberry, sumac, or other brushy vegetation. These birds nest quite late in the season, reflecting their dependence on late-maturing weed seeds. Three to four eggs are incubated by the female for about 12 days, and the young leave the nest from 8 to 14 days later.

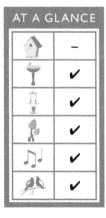

AT A GLANCE

🏠	–
🛁	✔
🏮	✔
🌹	✔
🎵	✔
🐦	✔

Red-winged Blackbird

For some folks, it just isn't summer without a male red-winged blackbird's loud conk-a-ree *song coming from a nearby field or marsh. Red-winged blackbirds are true harbingers of spring in many areas. The red-winged blackbird's name succinctly describes the male's handsome plumage, yet the females of this ubiquitous species have baffled many an observer. Their streaky brown plumage is confusingly sparrowlike. Studies have shown that one dominant male red-winged blackbird may have many adult females nesting in his territory. Red-winged blackbirds are present continent-wide for most of the year. Wet meadows, swamps, and salt marshes are common habitats for these birds, especially in spring and summer.*

HOW DO I IDENTIFY IT?   The *conk-a-ree* call of the male red-winged blackbird fills the air over marshes and fields all across North America. As he gives this call, announcing himself loudly to rivals and potential mates alike, he spreads his shoulders *just so,* showing bright red and yellow shoulder patches against his black wings. During winter, some people don't recognize these birds as red-winged blackbirds because the males aren't showing off those bright red wing patches. Redwings are medium-sized blackbirds (8¾ inches long) with an all-black body, an orange-red and yellow patch on the shoulder, and a nearly conical black bill. Females are streaky brown overall, but their longer bill helps distinguish them from the sparrows (which have stouter bills).

WHERE DO I FIND IT?   Look for these common blackbirds perched on telephone wires or cattails. Wet meadows, cattail marshes, upland grasslands, and pastures are all prime breeding habitat for red-winged blackbirds. In fall and winter, they may join with other blackbird species to form huge flocks. Northern nesting redwings migrate (starting in September and October) to the southern United States, while southern nesting birds are nonmigratory. Fall blackbird flocks move during the day in oblong, loose clouds of birds. These flocks forage by day in agricultural fields and are often persecuted as a nuisance species for the crop damage they inflict. Spring migration begins in mid-February and continues through mid-May.

WHAT CAN I FEED OR DO TO ATTRACT IT?   If you live on a farm or near any open fields or marshes, you have an excellent chance of attracting red-winged blackbirds to your feeders. The red-winged blackbird's diet is mostly plant matter—weed seeds, grain, sunflower seeds, and tree seeds—along with some insects, all of which are gleaned from the ground. They will also visit feeding stations for sunflower seeds, cracked corn, peanuts, and suet. These birds are most likely to visit feeders during harsh winter weather. Surprisingly, they are able to use a variety of feeder types. Red-winged blackbirds also relish the seeds from certain vines, such as trumpet vines.

NESTING   Nesting starts early for the red-winged blackbird, with males singing from an exposed perch in their territories as early as February in the South, later in the North. Females choose a nest site in a male's territory and build cup-shaped grass nests that are suspended from vertical supporting vegetation. Mud forms the foundation of the nest and soft grasses are the inner lining. Clutch size is three to four eggs, and the female alone incubates them for 10 to 13 days. Both parents care for the nestlings for about two weeks, until they are ready to leave the nest.

AT A GLANCE	
🏠	–
⚱	✔
🪣	✔
🌿	✔
🎵	✔
🐦	✔

Common Grackle

Grackles are large, conspicuous, and noisy birds that are equally at home in a town or country setting. This species benefited greatly from the European settlement of North America as forests were turned into farm fields and new feeding and nesting opportunities emerged for the common grackle. Residential areas and farmland are particularly attractive to grackles. Look for long, dark lines of migrating common grackles during the day, especially in fall. Migrating flocks can literally contain thousands of birds and may stretch from horizon to horizon. At feeders grackles relish cracked corn and sunflower seeds most of all. Grackles are also known to take hard, stale pieces of bread and dunk them in a birdbath to soften them.

HOW DO I IDENTIFY IT? Some beginning bird watchers will confuse grackles with starlings, but grackles are noticeably larger birds with much longer tails. In fact, nearly half of the common grackle's 12½-inch length is its tail. The grackle's black plumage is glossy and can show bright purple, bronze, or green highlights, especially on the head. Adult common grackles show a pale yellow eye, which contrasts sharply with their dark head. The powerful bill is long and sharply pointed. In flight, grackles hold their long tails in a "V," much like the keel of a boat. Males and females are very similar in appearance. In the West, you may also see the great-tailed grackle, a much larger species that looks like a common grackle on steroids. Grackles utter a variety of harsh, metallic-sounding tones.

WHERE DO I FIND IT? Common grackles are found in almost every habitat in eastern North America, though in winter the population is more concentrated in the eastern and southern United States. Grackles prefer edge habitat and open areas with scattered trees or shrubs. From late summer to early spring, grackles gather in large roosts with other blackbirds. These roosts can contain as many as half a million birds and are notable both for their noise and their droppings. Spring migrants may reach breeding territories as early as mid-February. Fall migration begins in September and peaks in October.

WHAT CAN I FEED OR DO TO ATTRACT IT? These birds will eat almost anything, so attracting them to a feeder is relatively easy—if you want to do that. Grackles will come to backyards for mixed seed, cracked corn, nuts, and sunflower hearts. During breeding season, grackles eat mostly insects, but they are opportunists and will take nestling birds or eggs, small fish, mice, and frogs. In winter the diet shifts to seeds and grain. The impact of foraging winter flocks on crops has earned the common grackle a reputation as an agricultural pest. Most of the grackle's foraging is done on the ground, where it tosses aside leaves and rubbish to uncover its food. Some people consider these birds backyard pests as well, as the grackles will often dominate the feeders and keep smaller birds from feeding.

NESTING Grackles prefer to nest in dense conifers, close to rich foraging habitat. The large, open cup nest is built by the female from grass, twigs, and mud and is lined with soft grass. She incubates the four to five eggs for about two weeks. The male joins her in feeding the nestlings an all-insect diet until fledging time arrives about 20 days later.

Brown-headed Cowbird

The cowbird's habit of laying its eggs in the nests of other, smaller songbirds makes the brown-headed cowbird a nest parasite. Cowbirds learned this behavior over centuries by following roaming herds of bison and cattle. The large mammals stirred up insects, the cowbird's main food. But all the movement made it impossible to stop, build a nest, and wait for the young to grow. So the cowbirds did the most convenient thing—they laid their eggs in any nest they could find along the way. Finding cowbirds is almost never a problem, but limiting their impact on our songbirds can be problematic. Many species are in serious decline because of cowbirds. One way to discourage cowbirds is to stop offering mixed seed and cracked corn during spring when they show up at bird feeders before many migratory songbirds return. If you see a songbird feeding a fledgling that is larger than the songbird, the fledgling is likely a cowbird.

HOW DO I IDENTIFY IT?   The cowbird is a smallish blackbird (7½ inches long). Males have a glossy black body and a dark brown head, while females are a dull gray-brown overall. The short, cone-shaped bill and pointed wings help to distinguish the brown-headed cowbird from larger blackbirds. The cowbird's song is a series of liquid gurgles followed by a high, thin whistle. It's an interesting, unique sound.

WHERE DO I FIND IT?   These birds are found just about everywhere in North America. In Canada and most of the northwestern United States, cowbirds are only present during the summer breeding season. Everywhere else, we have them year-round. Cowbirds are found in a variety of habitats, but they prefer woodland edges, brushy fields, and old pastures, though they are equally at home in city parks and suburban backyards. Forest fragmentation has allowed the cowbird to parasitize the nests of woodland species, such as thrushes and vireos. In winter, cowbirds often join flocks of other blackbirds—red-winged blackbirds, grackles, and European starlings—foraging in fields and grasslands and roosting en masse in large woodlots.

WHAT CAN I FEED OR DO TO ATTRACT IT?   Away from the backyard, cowbirds eat mostly weed and grass seeds, along with insects, especially grasshoppers and beetles. They readily visit feeders for mixed seed and cracked corn. Cowbirds prefer to eat on the ground but will sometimes come to tube feeders. As mentioned, many bird watchers and backyard enthusiasts want to avoid attracting these birds in order to help protect our other songbird species.

NESTING   Male cowbirds court females with a variety of songs, bows, and sky-pointing displays. When she is ready to lay an egg, the female finds a nest that often already contains the eggs of the nest's owner. This "host" nest is most frequently that of a smaller songbird—yellow warblers, song sparrows, red-eyed vireos, and chipping sparrows seem to be frequent victims—and the female cowbird may even remove one of the host's eggs before depositing her own. Hatchling cowbirds are almost always larger than their nest mates and are able to out-compete them for food, enhancing the cowbird's chances of survival. Fortunately, some bird species have evolved to recognize cowbird eggs and will build a new nest on top of the old one or will remove the cowbird egg before it hatches.

AT A GLANCE

🏠	–
🛁	✔
🌾	✔
🌱	–
🎵	✔
🐦	✔

Baltimore Oriole

The brilliant Baltimore oriole, like many long-distance migrants, leads three flamboyant lives: backyard, park, and forest nester in North America; winter nectar–fruit–and insect-eater in the tropics; and long-distance wanderer while moving between its two homes. Named for the colonial family that settled Maryland—the family crest of which sported this bird's striking orange and black colors—the Baltimore oriole is one of only two widespread eastern orioles. At one time, the Baltimore oriole was thought to belong to the same species as the Bullock's oriole of the West—they were both lumped together as the "northern oriole." You may be surprised to learn that orioles are actually blackbirds, which makes them closely related to birds like bobolinks, cowbirds, and red-winged blackbirds. Baltimore orioles proudly represent one state (Maryland, of course) and a certain popular baseball team. Well, I say "proudly," but then again, I doubt the birds have much of a say in the matter.

HOW DO I IDENTIFY IT? At rest and in flight, the male Baltimore oriole is a fireball of citrus orange blazed with black. This bird's head, its back, and much of its wings and tail are black. In flight, a bright orange shoulder and white wing bars flash, as do its orange tail corners. The female Baltimore oriole is also colorful, lacking the entirely black head of the male but having vibrant orange-yellow underparts. The Baltimore oriole usually reveals its presence with an unusually rich song and a clear, two-note whistle.

WHERE DO I FIND IT? During spring and fall migration, look for Baltimore orioles in open parklike woodlands, along forest edges, and in suburbs and city parks throughout the eastern United States. They prefer tall, mature trees, often in very open, widely scattered stands. They stay and nest throughout much of the East except in the southernmost states. Most of the population spends the winter from southern Mexico south to northwestern South America and in the Caribbean. Some Baltimore orioles winter in Florida.

WHAT CAN I FEED OR DO TO ATTRACT IT? Orioles are insect and fruit eaters, which means they won't come to seed feeders, but there are still plenty of ways you can attract these birds to your backyard. First, try expanding your backyard menu to include some of the Baltimore oriole's favorite entrées: orange and grapefruit halves, grape jelly, and sugar water. Special oriole feeders are available that make it very easy to offer these unique items at your feeding station. Second, plant berry-producing trees and shrubs—serviceberry is one good choice. Finally, you can never go wrong with a good birdbath. No bird can resist the sight and sound of moving water.

NESTING A female Baltimore oriole constructs a hanging, bag-shaped nest, sometimes with the help of her mate. Woven of plant fibers, string, and other materials, the nest hangs near the end of a large branch, usually between 20 and 30 feet off the ground. Try offering short pieces (2 inches or less) of string out in your yard for orioles to use in their nest construction. Within the enclosed nest, the female lays four or five bluish or grayish eggs, which are marked with brown and black. She incubates the eggs for about two weeks, and then both parents feed the nestlings, which leave the nest about two weeks after hatching.

AT A GLANCE	
🏠	–
⛲	✔
🪶	✔
🌺	✔
🎵	✔
🐦	✔

Purple Finch

The male purple finch is a rich raspberry-red (not purple) color and is often confused with the much more common male house finch (which is orange- or brick-red). Purple finches travel in flocks during the non-breeding seasons and may descend on feeding stations for a few hours or several weeks as they roam in search of a winter food source. In some areas, purple finches are in serious decline due to the more aggressive house finch. You may have both purple finches and house finches at your feeders, which means you have a great opportunity to learn to tell them apart. Once you see the differences in plumage (on males, check the distribution of the red; on females, check the facial pattern) you'll find that it's not that hard after all.

HOW DO I IDENTIFY IT?   "Like it was dipped headfirst in raspberry wine" is how many bird watchers describe the color of the male purple finch, and it's an apt description, because the raspberry color completely encircles the bird's upper body. On the smaller male house finch, the red covers only the head, face, and breast. The house finch's back and wings are brown and streaky. Large-headed with a stout bill, the purple finch is hard to miss, often announcing its arrival with a loud *pik!* call. Its song, which is sung beginning in late winter, is a loud, rich warble delivered from a treetop perch. Females are brown-backed with dark brown and white face patterns and dark cheek patches. Their white breasts are boldly streaked with brown.

WHERE DO I FIND IT?   These birds spend the summer throughout the northern boreal forests of Canada and then move into the eastern United States for the winter. They are year-round residents along the west coast and throughout the northeastern chunk of the United States. During the breeding season, you'll find purple finches in a variety of woodland habitats, from cool coniferous woods to deciduous forests, orchards, and edge habitat. During migration and in winter, they can be found almost anywhere in the eastern United States, from woodland edges to weedy fields and backyard feeding stations. They go wherever food is available and purple finch "invasions" in winter are often caused by shortages of natural food supplies in the North.

WHAT CAN I FEED OR DO TO ATTRACT IT?   Purple finches come to feeders for striped and black-oil sunflower seeds and thistle seed. Like most other finches, purple finches prefer tube feeders. Purple finches will also eat suet, peanut bits, and fruit. Away from the feeders, seeds, blossoms, buds, and fruits make up most of their diet, though they do eat insects. Favorite food trees include elms, tulip poplars, maples, dogwoods, sweet gums, sycamores, and ashes. Typical foraging involves a flock of purple finches ranging amid upper branches, grabbing and eating young buds. These birds are also attracted to moving water for drinking and bathing.

NESTING   Female purple finches do most of the nest building after the pair chooses a site in the outer branches of a large conifer tree. She weaves together bark strips, rootlets, and twigs into a cup and lines it with animal hair and fine grass. Three to seven eggs are deposited and incubated by the female for about two weeks. Both parents feed hatchlings until fledging time, about another two weeks later.

House Finch

Bird watchers who rely on an eastern field guide that is more than thirty years old may be forgiven for some confusion. This bird won't be in it! The house finch, native to the West, is a well established but recently arrived resident of the eastern United States. When legislation forbidding the trade of wild birds was passed in 1940, a small number of caged house finches were released on Long Island. These birds began to breed and the population exploded almost overnight. Now we have house finches galore across the eastern United States. These aggressive birds have put a lot of pressure on the closely related purple finch, a species that is now in serious decline in the East. Despite the negative connotations associated with these birds, house finches are colorful little birds that produce one of the most musical songs of our common backyard birds. Listen for the male singing persistently throughout the spring and summer from a nearby rooftop, telephone wire, or tall tree.

HOW DO I IDENTIFY IT?   People who feed birds are familiar with the house finches that sometimes cover feeders with fluttering, tweeting flocks. It's easy to see why they were kept as cage birds; the male's cheery, rich song, marked by a few harsh notes, tumbles brightly down the scale. Females are streaky, pale brown birds with white undersides; males have a rich pinkish red rump, head, and upper breast. By comparison, male purple finches have an overall "dipped in wine" look, with a reddish suffusion to their back and wings, while female purple finches are much more boldly streaked with brown and white than are female house finches. At first, many bird watchers struggle with keeping house and purple finches apart, but once you become familiar with these birds, the differences become more obvious.

WHERE DO I FIND IT?   As its name suggests, the house finch prefers nesting and feeding near homes. It's a thoroughly suburban bird in the East, but in its native West, it is found in undisturbed desert habitats as well. This species appears to be developing migratory behavior in the East, with a general movement toward the South in winter. House finches have also been introduced in Hawaii.

WHAT CAN I FEED OR DO TO ATTRACT IT?   For most feeding station proprietors, the question is not how to attract house finches, but how to discourage them. Even attractive birds with pleasant songs wear out their welcome when they descend in dozens, monopolizing feeders. Black-oil sunflower seeds are a favorite, closely followed by thistle and mixed seeds. Some people resort to removing perches from tube feeders, thus discouraging house finches, which are poor clingers. Most of the house finch's diet is vegetarian, and it spends a great deal of time feeding on the ground. Weed seeds, buds, and fruits are its mainstays away from feeding stations.

AT A GLANCE	
	—
	✔
	✔
	✔
	✔
	✔
	✔

NESTING   House finch nests are shallow twig platforms with a finely woven inner cup composed of rootlets, grass, feathers, and string. They are tucked into dense ornamental evergreens, hanging baskets, ledges, ivy-covered walls, and other nooks where there is an overhanging structure. Two to five eggs are incubated by the female, while the male feeds her. Young are fed regurgitated seeds and fledge from 12 to 16 days later.

Pine Siskin

This slender, streaky little finch is often overlooked—mistaken for a female house finch, a winter-plumaged goldfinch, or just "a little brown bird." But a closer look reveals a slender-billed, finely streaked finch adorned with yellow in its wings and tail. Though commonly found throughout the United States each winter, pine siskins are among those northern finch species—along with crossbills, redpolls, and evening grosbeaks—that periodically invade the United States from the far North in large numbers. What happens is the normal food supply (forest seed crops) in the northern forests suffers a dramatic decline and forces the birds to travel widely in search of abundant supplies. If you have a well-stocked feeding station, you may see large flocks of siskins in your backyard during invasion winters. Thistle seed (nyjer) is a favorite of pine siskins.

HOW DO I IDENTIFY IT? Your first clue to a pine siskin's presence may be its loud, descending *tzeeeew!* call as a flock drops into your backyard trees. Siskins also give a rising *zweeeeet!* sound and sing a jumbled twitter of notes similar to a goldfinch's song. Fine brown streaks cover the pine siskin's body, but as the bird moves, its yellow wing stripes and tail spots flash—a surprise bit of color on this otherwise drab bird.

WHERE DO I FIND IT? Across the Midwest and the eastern United States the pine siskin is a winter visitor. It nests in the coniferous forests of the far North and throughout the West but makes nearly annual appearances throughout eastern North America. During spring and summer, pine siskins are never far from conifers, alders, and the mixed woodlands in which they breed and forage. In winter, siskins often move southward—sometimes in great numbers—in search of food. They forage in weedy fields, hedgerows, and pine woods and at backyard feeding stations. Listen for the sharp, zippy calls of siskin flocks as they fly over. And be sure to look carefully at your flocks of drab winter goldfinches—a siskin may be accompanying them.

WHAT CAN I FEED OR DO TO ATTRACT IT? Add a thistle feeder and seed to your backyard offerings and you'll increase your chances of attracting siskins. Look for these tiny seeds wherever you buy wild bird supplies. You can also obtain feeders specifically designed for thistle seed. Siskins are also attracted to sunflower bits. Siskins eat grass and weed seeds, especially wild thistle seeds, plus tree buds, pine seeds, berries, and some insects. Expert clingers, siskins will hang upside-down on a catkin clump, pinecone, or weed stem and pry seeds loose with their finely pointed bills. Pine siskins readily come to birdbaths with moving water.

NESTING Male siskins begin courting females in late winter, before reaching their breeding grounds, as the winter feeding flocks are dispersing. Siskins are known to nest in loose colonies in conifer or mixed conifer-deciduous forests. The female builds the cup-shaped nest out of weed stems, grasses, bark strips, vines, and rootlets and lines it with soft material like animal fur, feathers, thistledown, or moss. She lays three to five eggs and incubates them for about two weeks, during which time the male may bring her food. Both parents feed the nestlings, which leave the nest about 15 days after hatching.

AT A GLANCE

	–
	✔
	✔
	✔
	✔
	✔

American Goldfinch

The bright canary-yellow and black plumage of the breeding male American goldfinch has earned this species the nickname "wild canary." These birds are familiar visitors to bird feeders at all seasons, especially in winter, though they may go unnoticed when dressed in their drab winter garb. The goldfinch's undulating flight is accompanied by a twittering call of perchickoree or potato chip! Goldfinches love to drink and bathe in shallow birdbaths and are especially attracted to moving water.

HOW DO I IDENTIFY IT? American goldfinches appear very different in summer and winter. The male's brilliant yellow body and black cap in summer give way to a drab, olive-brown plumage in winter. Female goldfinches, though never bright yellow, also lose most of their color. Both sexes retain their black wings and tail year-round. The sweet, high-pitched, warbling song of the male is often given in early spring, just as these small (5-inch-long) birds are beginning to show their first bright yellow feathers.

WHERE DO I FIND IT? The twittering calls of goldfinches will alert you to the presence of these energetic songbirds. Weedy fields, brushy woodland edges, and open habitats with scattered shrubs are the American goldfinch's normal habitats. In the breeding season, they prefer weedy fields with thistles and other seed-producing plants. In winter, goldfinches roam in noisy flocks, seeking food in fields, in gardens, and at backyard feeding stations. These birds are common throughout the United States and southern Canada.

WHAT CAN I FEED OR DO TO ATTRACT IT? The secret to attracting goldfinches to your yard is thistle (nyjer) seed. Look for these tiny seeds wherever you buy wild bird supplies. You can also obtain feeders specifically designed for thistle seed. Hang a few thistle feeders in your backyard and you will likely have goldfinches year-round. These birds also visit for sunflower seeds and peanut bits. Goldfinches are seed-eaters in all seasons, and away from the feeders they consume a huge variety of weed, grass, and plant seeds as well as tree buds. They are attracted to many backyard plants and weeds, including thistles (of course), goldenrods, and dandelions. Goldfinches are agile birds, able to exploit seed sources that other finches cannot by hanging upside-down from seedheads, plant stalks, and bird feeders.

NESTING Goldfinches' nesting season begins late, an adaptation to ensure that nesting occurs when there is the greatest natural abundance of seeds, as well as the soft thistledown that goldfinches use to line their nests. Late June is the earliest nesting time, but peak nesting season is late July, and some nesting occurs as late as September. The site is in a shaded spot in a sapling or shrub and is selected by the pair. The female builds the open cup nest from twigs (attached with spider web), rootlets, and plant stems, and she lines it with soft thistledown or a similarly soft material. Four to six eggs are incubated by the female for about two weeks, with the male bringing food to her on the nest. Both parents tend the nestlings for 12 to 17 days before they fledge. Goldfinches do not fall victim to brown-headed cowbirds, as young cowbirds are unable to survive the all-seed diet fed to nestling goldfinches.

AT A GLANCE	
	–
	✔
	✔
	✔
	✔
	✔

House Sparrow

This is that common little brown bird that you see on city sidewalks, around traffic lights, in shopping mall parking lots, and sometimes inside the shopping mall itself. They're everywhere. Given the abundance of house sparrows today, you might be surprised to learn that less than two hundred years ago there were no house sparrows in North America at all. The birds were introduced here from England in the 1850s to help control wireworms. The house sparrow population spread from a few birds in New York to the entire North American continent in just fifty years. It is one of the world's most successful and widespread species.

HOW DO I IDENTIFY IT?   The chunky little house sparrow is known for its constant *cha-deep, cha-deep* calls and for the male's black bib in breeding plumage. Breeding males have a black bill and a contrasting black, gray, and brown head and face pattern. Winter males are a muted version of the breeding plumage. Females are drab gray-brown overall and lack the bib. House sparrows are constantly chirping and are aggressive competitors at feeders and nest sites.

WHERE DO I FIND IT?   House sparrows are year-round residents. It's easier to describe where you *won't* find house sparrows because they are practically ubiquitous. Pristine natural habitats—forest, grassland, or desert—that lack human development will also lack house sparrows. Historically, the house sparrow associated with horses (and the seeds and insects in their droppings) and other livestock. Today, house sparrows are found in the most urban of habitats, living on food scraps and nesting in building crevices—though they're still commonly found in horse barns, farmyards, and feedlots.

WHAT CAN I FEED OR DO TO ATTRACT IT?   House sparrows are feeding station regulars, especially in towns and cities. Seeds and grains will be on the house sparrow's normal menu throughout the year. In spring and summer, they take advantage of bountiful insect populations. At any time, house sparrows are quick to take food at bird feeders or scraps of food offered directly or indirectly by humans in parks, picnic areas, fast food restaurants, and strip malls. Cracked corn, sunflower seeds, peanut bits, and bread products are favorite foods. Truth be told, if you're one of the few people in America who does not have house sparrows in the backyard, you might want to consider yourself lucky and try to keep it that way. These birds are very aggressive and tend to dominate any backyard feeding station, driving away your other songbirds.

NESTING   Males choose a cavity and sing by it to attract the female. Both build the messy nest of grass, weed stems, feathers, paper, and string. The female lays between three and six eggs, which are incubated by both parents for 10 or more days. The parents share feeding duties until the nestlings are ready to fledge at about two weeks. House sparrows often steal nest boxes from bluebirds, swallows, and purple martins (forcing many nest box landlords to use controls and special housing to discourage house sparrows), and they sometimes even kill nest box competitors. To discourage house sparrows from dominating nest boxes, use boxes with interiors less than 5 inches deep, remove their nesting material regularly, and place nest boxes far from buildings and thick shrubbery.

AT A GLANCE	
🏠	✔
⛲	✔
🕯	✔
🌿	✔
♪♩	✔
🐦	✔

Beyond the Backyard
Birding Hotspots
for the Midwest

Prairie Ridge State Natural Area/Newton Lake State Fish and Wildlife Area
(year-round)
4295 N. 100th Street
Newton, IL 62448
(618) 783-2685

This is the place to see the rare greater prairie chicken put on its fascinating courtship display. In March and April, nature lovers join guided tours to visit these state-owned lands in southeastern Illinois to watch the prairie chickens from viewing blinds at dawn. This 1,700-acre site of woodlands, grasslands, meadows, wetlands, and agricultural fields also attracts other rare species to breed, including loggerhead shrike, northern harrier, short-eared owl, and Henslow's sparrow. Year-round, look for northern mockingbirds, and in winter, watch for rough-legged hawks. In winter, you might also enjoy watching the "changing of the guard" at dusk as northern harriers finish feeding for the day while short-eared owls move in on their territory to begin the nighttime hunt. In spring and summer, you can find plenty of wading birds in the marshes, and at the large cooling lake, ducks and other migratory waterfowl abound.

Hawk Ridge Nature Preserve
(fall)
P.O. Box 3006
Duluth, MN 55803
(218) 428-6209
www.hawkridge.org

Hawk Ridge is likely Minnesota's most famous birding site and for good reason—some of Minnesota's most-watched birds fly over the reserve. On September 15, 2003, more than 102,000 raptors were counted passing over Hawk Ridge. The record total on that famed day included more than 101,000 broad-winged hawks. The National Audubon Society has named Hawk Ridge an Important Bird Area. The vastness of Lake Superior creates a natural barrier that birds are reluctant to fly over and this causes southbound migrants to funnel over Hawk Ridge. Flocks (kettles) of hawks ride the updrafts of warm air that form along the ridges running parallel to the shore of the lake. Cold fronts with winds from the northwest or west make for impressive numbers of birds, with the peak migration typically occurring in mid-September. October is a good time to see bald and golden eagles, red-tailed hawks, and northern goshawks. Most of the hawks tend to fly past during the first couple hours after sunrise, and the activity slows down in mid-afternoon. There are not a lot of raptors on the wing on rainy and foggy days when the wind is calm.

Sax-Zim Bog
(year-round)
Forest Ecologist DNR
2005 Highway 37
Eveleth, MN 55734
(218) 744-7447
www.sax-zimbog.com

Many a birder has said that if they could bird in only one spot in Minnesota, they would choose Sax-Zim Bog. Located in St. Louis County, this accessible conifer bog offers nesting great gray owls, Connecticut warblers, gray jays, upland sandpipers, sharp-tailed and ruffed grouse, yellow-bellied flycatchers, evening grosbeaks, and boreal chickadees. Other summer possibilities include pine and golden-winged warblers; white-crowned, clay-colored, Le Conte's, and white-throated sparrows; sedge and winter wrens; alder flycatcher; and black-billed magpie. The great gray owl is a year-round resident in this 200-square-mile mix of spruce, cedar, and tamarack bogs. During winter, the bogs are good places to look for great gray owl, northern hawk-owl, and snowy owl, northern goshawks, redpolls, grosbeaks, crossbills, black-backed woodpeckers, and northern shrike. Sax-Zim is named for its proximity to two small towns that are, as you might guess, named Sax and Zim.

Horicon National Wildlife Refuge
(fall)
W4279 Headquarters Road
Mayville, WI 53050
(920) 387-2658
www.midwest.fws.gov/Horicon

Regarded by many as Wisconsin's premier bird-watching spot, Horicon Marsh made the list of American Bird Conservancy's Globally Important Bird Areas. Dubbed "the Everglades of the North," this 32,000-acre restored marshland is the largest freshwater cattail marsh in the United States. Horicon is the largest stopover site for migrant Canada geese in the Midwest, with peak one-day counts of 200,000 during the fall, and also serves as the largest nesting grounds for redheads east of the Mississippi. The refuge receives about 400,000 human visitors a year, many during fall migration. Six miles of hiking trails and an auto tour provide good viewing opportunities within the refuge; many birders also pull off the road along Highway 49 east of Waupun to scan the marsh for teal, wigeons, pintails, and other waterfowl. Great egrets are common in the refuge, with cattle and snowy egrets sometimes found in late summer. Little blue and tricolored herons are less common. Records exist for American avocet, black-necked stilt, glossy ibis, and black-bellied whistling duck—all rare in Wisconsin. Look and listen for soras and other rails along the Egret Trail, a floating boardwalk. Bobolinks and dickcissels breed in grassy areas within the refuge, with yellow-headed blackbirds and American white pelicans also among the summer residents.

Whitefish Point Bird Observatory
(spring and fall)
16914 North Whitefish Point Road
Paradise, MI 49768
(906) 492-3596
www.wpbo.org

Located in Michigan's eastern Upper Peninsula, the Whitefish Point area is famous throughout the Upper Midwest for its impressive waterbird migrations as well as its proven attraction as a vagrant trap. In spring and fall, significant flights of loons, grebes, and ducks, including scoters and long-tailed ducks, can be observed from the beach at the tip of the point near the waterbird shack. Especially in fall, there may be no better place in the region for seeing migrant jaegers. In spring, hawks migrate along the point, with a highlight in April being the numbers of rough-legged hawks. Owls also use this area during migration, and Whitefish Point is one of the better sites in the state for migrating northern saw-whet and long-eared owls and for rare irruptives, including boreal, great gray, and northern hawk owls. Numerous songbirds also migrate along the point, and the bird checklist for the area exceeds three hundred species. Nearby patches of boreal forest hold other resident species of interest, including spruce grouse, black-backed wood-pecker, gray jay, and boreal chickadee. In many winters, pine grosbeaks, red- and white-winged crossbills, common redpolls, pine siskins, and evening grosbeaks can be found in the area.

Seney National Wildlife Refuge
(spring and summer)
HCR #2, Box 1
Seney, MI 49883
(906) 586-9851
www.midwest.fws.gov/Seney/VisInfo.htm

With approximately 5,000 acres of bogs, marshes, swamps, grasslands, and forest, the Seney National Wildlife Refuge provides excellent bird-watching opportunities from spring through fall. Breeding Le Conte's sparrows (rare) and yellow rails (listed as threatened on state lists) can be found in the area's sedge marshes. This is the primary site where trumpeter swans were introduced into Michigan, and the state's largest breeding population is found here. Boreal habitats are home to black-backed woodpeckers, gray jays, boreal chickadees, and great gray owls. In the grassland areas, sharp-tailed grouse can be found in early May. The main vehicle access is from the 7-mile Marshland Drive, where many migrants and breeding waterbirds can be seen, including common loons, American bitterns, and sandhill cranes. The 1.4-mile Pine Ridge Nature Trail passes through wetland and forested habitats where a variety of breeding warblers, vireos, thrushes, and sparrows may be found. Evening tours are conducted to see the elusive yellow rail in May.

Squaw Creek National Wildlife Refuge
(fall through spring)
Refuge Manager
P.O. Box 158
Mound City, MO 64470
(660) 442-3187
www.fws.gov/midwest/SquawCreek

Squaw Creek is located 90 minutes north of Kansas City just off Interstate 29. Take Missouri Highway 159 west at exit 79 for two miles to the headquarters and entrance. For sheer numbers of birds, few places in the United States can match Squaw Creek in fall and spring, when up to 400,000 snow geese will stop. A ten-mile loop drive runs through pools of cattails, lotus, arrowhead, and past mudflats, open fields, old woodlands, meadows, and scrub habitat. In winter the refuge hosts several hundred bald eagles. Ross's geese can be found in the snow goose flocks, and as many as 8 million blackbirds have been logged on Christmas Bird Counts. Harlan's red-tailed hawks are common here in winter, as are short-eared owls. In spring migration, all three phalarope species can be seen. In summer, least bitterns, yellow-headed blackbirds, and great-tailed grackles breed here.

Magee Marsh Wildlife Area
(spring)
13229 West State Route 2
Oak Harbor, OH 43449
(419) 898-0960
www.dnr.state.oh.us/wildlife/Hunting/wildlifeareas/northwest/northwa.htm

The Magee Marsh Wildlife Area, along with the nearby Ottawa National Wildlife Refuge, has hosted more than three hundred bird species. Part of the vast western Lake Erie marshland ecosystem, Magee contains a diversity of wetlands, woodlots, and beaches that buffer the open waters of Lake Erie. The centerpiece of the site is the legendary "Bird Trail." This half-mile-long elevated boardwalk traverses a 7-acre swamp woods. Catch the right day in May and the trees seem to drip with brightly colored jewels—warblers, vireos, tanagers, orioles, grosbeaks, and other brilliant neotropical migrants. The main road through the wildlife area passes through one of the finest Ohio marshes, and ducks, geese, and other water birds abound and are readily observed from the roadway. Watch closely for American bitterns; they are often seen along the road. Bald eagles are frequently seen hunting over the marshes. Magee is on a major hawk flyway, and March is the best time to observe this phenomenon. Not far from the interesting Sportsmen's Migratory Bird Center is a large, elevated tower built specifically to enhance viewing of raptors passing overhead. This post offers a commanding view of the surrounding marshes, and on a good day, several hundred raptors might be tallied.

Reelfoot National Wildlife Refuge
(year-round)
4343 Highway 157
Union City, TN 38261
(731) 538-2481
www.fws.gov/reelfoot

This refuge includes some 25,000 acres of open water, close to 2,000 acres of bottomland forests, and many acres of croplands in both Kentucky and Tennessee. Birding is excellent almost anytime of year at Reelfoot. The lake and its surroundings are not only regular stopovers for millions of migrating birds in spring and fall, but they are also breeding grounds for a number of neotropical migrant species. Ospreys, wood thrushes, prothonotary warblers, hooded mergansers, wood ducks, and red-shouldered hawks nest here along with many others. The red-headed woodpecker is resident here along with five other woodpeckers commonly found in the South year-round; the yellow-bellied sapsucker winters here. More than a half-million ducks and geese winter on the refuge along with more than 200 bald eagles. Although the refuge lands are closed to the public from March 15 to November 15, the auto-tour route is open year-round and many other nearby areas are accessible.

Birds I've Spotted

Species/Description: _____

Date/Time of Day: _____

Location (at a feeder? birdhouse?): _____

Special Notes: _____

Species/Description: _____

Date/Time of Day: _____

Location (at a feeder? birdhouse?): _____

Special Notes: _____

Species/Description: _____

Date/Time of Day: _____

Location (at a feeder? birdhouse?): _____

Special Notes: _____

Species/Description: _____

Date/Time of Day: _____

Location (at a feeder? birdhouse?): _____

Special Notes: _____

Species/Description: _____

Date/Time of Day: _____

Location (at a feeder? birdhouse?): _____

Special Notes: _____

Species/Description: _____

Date/Time of Day: _____

Location (at a feeder? birdhouse?): _____

Special Notes: _____

Species/Description: _____

Date/Time of Day: _____

Location (at a feeder? birdhouse?): _____

Special Notes: _____

Species/Description: _____

Date/Time of Day: _____

Location (at a feeder? birdhouse?): _____

Special Notes: _____

Species/Description: _____

Date/Time of Day: _____

Location (at a feeder? birdhouse?): _____

Special Notes: _____

Species/Description: _____

Date/Time of Day: _____

Location (at a feeder? birdhouse?): _____

Special Notes: _____

Species/Description: _____

Date/Time of Day: _____

Location (at a feeder? birdhouse?): _____

Special Notes: _____

Species/Description: _____

Date/Time of Day: _____

Location (at a feeder? birdhouse?): _____

Special Notes: _____

Resources

ORGANIZATIONS

American Bird Conservancy
P.O. Box 249
4249 Loudoun Avenue
The Plains, VA 20198-2237
www.abcbirds.org

American Birding Association
P.O. Box 6599
Colorado Springs, CO 80934-6599
800-850-2473
www.americanbirding.org

Cornell Laboratory of Ornithology
159 Sapsucker Woods Road
Ithaca, NY 14850
800-843-2473
www.birds.cornell.edu

National Audubon Society
225 Varick Street
New York, NY 10014
www.audubon.org/bird/at_home/
HealthyYard_BirdHabitat.html

National Wildlife Federation
Backyard Habitat Program
11100 Wildlife Center Drive
Reston, VA 20190
www.nwf.org/Get-Outside/Outdoor-
Activities/Garden-for-Wildlife.aspx

**The National Wildlife
Rehabilitators Association**
2625 Clearwater Road, Suite 110
St. Cloud, MN 56301
www.nwrawildlife.org/content/
finding-rehabilitator

The Nature Conservancy
4245 North Fairfax Drive #100
Arlington, VA 22203
www.nature.org

North American Bluebird Society
P.O. Box 7844
Bloomington, IN 47407
www.nabluebirdsociety.org

North American Native Plant Society
P.O. Box 84, Station D
Etobicoke, ON M9A 4X1
Canada
www.nanps.org

**Purple Martin
Conservation Association**
301 Peninsula Drive, Suite 6
Erie, PA 16505
www.purplemartin.org

The Purple Martin Society
www.purplemartins.com

PERIODICALS FOR BIRD WATCHERS

Bird Watcher's Digest
P.O. Box 110
Marietta, OH 45750
800-879-2473
www.birdwatchersdigest.com

Watching Backyard Birds Newsletter
P.O. Box 110
Marietta, OH 45750
800-879-2473
www.watchingbackyardbirds.com

Living Bird
Cornell Laboratory of Ornithology
159 Sapsucker Woods Road
Ithaca, NY 14850
800-843-2473
www.birds.cornell.edu

Index

Meet Bill Thompson III

Bill Thompson III has been a bird watcher for more than forty years—much of it in his own backyard. From an early age he knew his life would be intertwined with birds and bird watching; in fact, his grand-mother claimed his first word as a baby was "junco." The bird that got him started as a bird watcher was a lone snowy owl that visited his family's Iowa yard when Bill was just seven years old. From that magic moment, Bill has never stopped watching birds for long.

Bill is the editor and co-publisher of *Bird Watcher's Digest,* a magazine started by his family in 1978 in Marietta, Ohio. He is the author of numerous books on birds and nature, including the award-winning *Young Birder's Guide to Birds of North America.* In great demand as a speaker, birding guide, and performer, Bill has watched birds in forty-nine states and more than thirty countries. He is currently vice president and a founding board member of the Ohio Ornithological Society.

Bill lives with his wife, author/artist Julie Zickefoose, and their two children on 80 acres of wooded farmland in Whipple, Ohio. To date, Bill and family have seen and identified 186 bird species on their farm, many of which were attracted to the bird-friendly habitat that Bill and Julie have created there. When he's not birding or traveling in search of birds, Bill enjoys recording and performing with his country rock band the Rain Crows.

You can catch up with Bill via these birdy channels:
Bird Watcher's Digest: www.birdwatchersdigest.com
Bill of the Birds blog: www.billofthebirds.blogspot.com
Twitter: @billofthebirds, @bwdmag
Facebook: Bird Watcher's Digest

Printed in the USA
CPSIA information can be obtained
at www.ICGtesting.com
LVHW070103080824
787688LV00015BA/475